Financial Management for Rehab Leaders

A Practical Guide

David Potach

davidpotach.com

For my family...

Contents

Author's Note

As a physical therapist with over two decades of experience in both clinical and leadership roles, I have witnessed firsthand the rapid evolution of healthcare finance. When I first stepped into a management position, I quickly realized that my clinical training, while helpful, had not fully prepared me for the financial responsibilities that came with leading a rehab department.

Like many of my colleagues, I grappled with budgets, reimbursement models, and revenue cycle management—concepts that were far removed from the hands-on patient care I was accustomed to. It was a steep learning curve, and I often wished for a comprehensive resource that could guide me through the complexities of rehab finance.

That's what inspired me to write this book. "Rehab Department Finances: A Comprehensive Guide for Rehabilitation Leaders" is the culmination of years of experience, research, and collaboration with experts in the field. My goal is to provide rehabilitation professionals with a practical, accessible, and comprehensive resource that bridges the gap between clinical expertise and financial acumen.

Throughout the book, you'll follow the story of Amanda, a physical therapist who has recently transitioned into a leadership role as the director of a rehab department. Like many of us, Amanda faces the challenge of navigating the complex world of healthcare finance while still maintaining her commitment to providing exceptional patient care.

As Amanda tackles each new financial concept and challenge, you'll learn alongside her, gaining the knowledge and skills necessary to make informed decisions and drive positive change in your own practice. From mastering the basics of accounting and budgeting to exploring advanced topics like revenue cycle management and leading financial change, Amanda's journey will serve as a relatable and engaging framework for your own learning.

One of the key features of this book is its focus on real-life scenarios and case studies. Throughout the chapters, you'll see Amanda apply her newfound knowledge to situations that mirror the challenges you face in your own practice. Whether you're working in a hospital-based rehab department or a private clinic, you'll find relevant examples and exercises that will help you cement your understanding of the concepts.

Another important aspect of this book is its emphasis on the interconnectedness of clinical outcomes, financial performance, and operational efficiency. As Amanda navigates her new role, she learns these elements cannot be viewed in isolation. By understanding how they influence and impact each other, she becomes a more effective leader, making holistic, data-driven decisions that benefit her patients, her team, and her organization.

Writing this book has been a labor of love, and I am deeply grateful to the many colleagues, mentors, and industry experts who have shared their insights and experiences with me along the way. Their contributions have enriched the content and ensured that the information presented is both accurate and relevant to the current healthcare landscape.

It is my sincere hope that "Rehab Department Finances" becomes a valuable resource for rehabilitation professionals at all stages of their careers. Whether you are a recent graduate stepping into your first leadership role or a seasoned director looking to enhance your financial skills, this book meets you where you are and provides you with the tools and knowledge you need to succeed.

As you embark on this learning journey alongside Amanda, I encourage you to approach the material with an open mind and a willingness to apply the concepts to your own practice. Share your insights and experiences with your colleagues, and never hesitate to reach out for support when you need it. Together, we can build a stronger, more financially savvy rehabilitation community that is well-equipped to face the challenges and opportunities of the future.

With that, I invite you to turn the page and begin your exploration of the world of rehab finance. I am confident that the knowledge and skills you gain from this book, and from Amanda's relatable experiences, will serve you well throughout your career and help you make a lasting, positive impact on the lives of your patients and the success of your organization.

you make a lasting positive impact on the lives of your patients and the success of your

Preface

Imagine this scenario: After years of hard work and dedication as a physical therapist, you finally land your dream job as the Director of Rehabilitation Services at a respected hospital. You're thrilled about this new opportunity to lead a team of skilled clinicians and make a positive impact on patient care. However, on your very first day, your boss, the hospital's Vice President of Operations, stops by your office with a serious concern.

"I've been reviewing our financial reports, and I noticed that our net patient service revenue for the rehab department is significantly lower than expected," she explains. "I need you to dive into the budget and help determine what's causing this issue. We need to get this sorted out quickly."

Your heart sinks. As an experienced clinician, you're confident in your ability to provide exceptional patient care and lead a team of therapists. But the business side of healthcare? That's a foreign concept to you. Suddenly, you face a daunting challenge that your clinical training never quite prepared you for.

If this situation sounds all too familiar, you're not alone. Many rehabilitation professionals excel in their clinical roles but feel ill-equipped to navigate the complex financial landscape of healthcare. That's precisely where this book comes in.

"Financial Management for Rehab Leaders: A Practical Guide" bridges the gap between your clinical expertise and the financial knowledge you need to thrive in your leadership role. This book will guide you through the ins and outs of rehabilitation finance across various settings, including hospital-based departments and private clinics.

Throughout the chapters, we'll tackle real-life scenarios and challenges that rehabilitation leaders face every day. You'll learn how to:

- Interpret and analyze financial statements to identify areas for improvement

- Develop and manage budgets that align with your department's goals and resources

- Understand various reimbursement methodologies and their impact on revenue

- Implement strategies to optimize therapist productivity and documentation

- Navigate the revenue cycle process to ensure timely and accurate payments

- Explore new revenue streams and service line opportunities for growth

- Make data-driven decisions that balance financial sustainability with clinical excellence

By mastering these critical financial concepts and their practical applications, you'll be well-equipped to lead your rehabilitation department to success. You'll learn how to speak the language of finance confidently, collaborate effectively with administrative colleagues, and make informed decisions that benefit both your patients and your organization.

But this book goes beyond just teaching you the basics of rehab finance. Each chapter infuses real-world examples, case studies, and practical exercises, bringing the concepts to life. You'll apply your newfound knowledge to scenarios that mirror the challenges you face in your own department.

As you progress through the chapters, you'll develop a comprehensive understanding of how clinical outcomes, financial performance, and operational efficiency are interconnected. You'll discover how to leverage this knowledge to drive positive change, innovate service delivery, and position your department for long-term success in the ever-evolving healthcare landscape.

Whether you're a new director like the one in our opening scenario or a seasoned leader looking to enhance your financial acumen, this book is your go-to resource. By combining essential financial concepts with practical, rehab-specific applications, "Financial Management for Rehab Leaders" empowers you to lead with confidence and make a lasting impact on the lives of your patients and the success of your organization.

So, let's dive in and embark on this journey together. With each chapter, you'll gain the tools and insights you need to navigate the complex world of rehab finance and emerge as a more effective, well-rounded leader. Your dream job awaits, and with the knowledge gained from this book, you'll be ready to tackle any financial challenge that comes your way.

Introduction

Dear reader, please meet Amanda, a physical therapist with ten years of clinical experience who's traded in her khaki pants for a fancy new title: Director of Rehab Services at Bayview Medical Center. She's got a sparkle in her eye and a spring in her step, ready to take on the world of healthcare finance. Little does she know, she's about to embark on a wild ride filled with budgets, spreadsheets, and enough acronyms to make her head spin.

As Amanda settles into her new office, complete with a slightly lopsided "World's Best Boss" mug, she can't help but feel a mix of excitement and terror when she realizes that her clinical expertise hasn't fully prepared her for the financial responsibilities of her position. During her first meeting with the hospital's CFO, Mark Thompson, Amanda learned her new position isn't just about making patients' muscles work again; it's also about making sure the department's finances are as healthy

as a triathlete. "Amanda, your role as director
of rehab is crucial not only for delivering excellent patient care but also for ensuring the
financial sustainability of your department,"
Mark explained. "I'm here to support you in
navigating this new terrain and making informed financial decisions."

The healthcare industry is undergoing a significant transformation, driven by changing
patient expectations, technological advancements, regulatory pressures, and the shift towards value-based care. Rehabilitation services, an essential component of the healthcare
continuum, are not immune to these changes. Rehab leaders today face a complex and
evolving financial landscape that requires a deep understanding of business principles and
strategic decision-making skills to navigate successfully.

In recent years, the rehab sector has experienced several key trends and challenges that
have direct implications for financial management:

1. Transition to Value-Based Reimbursement: Payers are increasingly moving away
   from traditional fee-for-service models that reward volume and towards value-based systems that tie reimbursement to patient outcomes, quality, and
   cost-efficiency. This shift requires rehab leaders to focus on demonstrating the
   value of their services and optimizing care delivery to maximize both clinical
   results and financial sustainability.

2. Increasing Cost Pressures: Rehab providers face mounting pressure to control
   costs in the face of tightening reimbursement rates, rising operating expenses,
   and heightened competition. Leaders must streamline operations, eliminate
   waste, and allocate resources effectively to maintain profitability without compromising care quality.

3. Regulatory Compliance: Healthcare is a heavily regulated industry, and rehab
   leaders must stay current with an ever-changing landscape of rules and requirements. From coding and billing regulations to quality reporting mandates,
   compliance burdens can significantly impact financial performance if not man-

aged proactively.

4. Workforce Challenges: Attracting and retaining skilled rehab professionals is an ongoing challenge, particularly in a tight labor market. Leaders must balance the need for competitive compensation and benefits with budget constraints, while also investing in staff development and engagement to drive productivity and care quality.

5. Technology Investments: The rapid pace of technological change presents both opportunities and challenges for rehab organizations. From electronic health records to telehealth platforms to robotic-assisted therapies, technology can enhance care delivery and operational efficiency. However, rehab organizations must carefully evaluate and justify these investments, as they often require significant upfront costs and ongoing maintenance.

6. Market Consolidation: The rehab sector is experiencing a wave of mergers, acquisitions, and partnerships as providers seek economies of scale, bargaining power, and integrated care delivery models. Leaders must navigate the financial complexities of these transactions while ensuring strategic alignment and cultural fit.

To thrive in this dynamic environment, rehab leaders must possess a strong foundation in financial management principles. This includes understanding key concepts like budgeting, reimbursement methodologies, productivity measures, revenue cycle management, and capital planning. Equally important are the strategic skills to make data-driven decisions, adapt to changing market conditions, and communicate effectively with diverse stakeholders.

This book aims to equip rehab leaders with the financial acumen and practical tools needed to drive fiscal sustainability and clinical excellence in their organizations. By mastering these skills, leaders can position their teams to navigate the challenges ahead and seize opportunities for growth and innovation. Financial expertise is no longer a nice-to-have for rehab leaders; it is a core competency for success in the modern healthcare landscape.

As Amanda settles into her new role, she can't help but reflect on the journey ahead. "I may not have all the answers yet," she thinks, "but I'm ready to learn, to grow, and to lead this department to success, one spreadsheet at a time."

Personal Reflection: Amanda realizes that taking on a leadership role means embracing both the challenges and the opportunities that come with it. She knows that success will require a willingness to learn, a positive attitude, and a commitment to her team and patients. With a deep breath and a smile, she dives in, ready to tackle whatever comes her way.

Chapter One

Accounting

Amanda dives headfirst into the world of financial reports and accounting jargon, feeling like she's landed on an alien planet where everyone speaks in numbers. She's pretty sure that "EBITDA" isn't a trendy new yoga pose, but she's determined to figure it out. In a meeting with the finance manager, Brooklyn Davis, Amanda decides to embrace her inner accountant.

"Brooklyn, I feel like I need a decoder ring to understand these financial statements," Amanda confesses, holding up a report covered in more highlighter than a college textbook.

Brooklyn laughs, "Don't worry, Amanda. It's not as complicated as it seems. Let's break it down together, and soon you'll be fluent in the language of debits and credits."

As they pore over the statements, Amanda starts to see the story behind the numbers. She even spots a few opportunities for improvement, like cutting back on the department's monthly supply of novelty stress balls.

A ccounting is a critical component of managing the financial health of a rehabilitation practice. Accounting provides the quantitative information needed to make informed business decisions. This chapter will cover some basics of accounting relevant for rehabilitation managers, including financial versus managerial accounting, essential financial statements, financial analysis methods, and key accounting ratios.

Financial vs. Managerial Accounting

There are two main branches of accounting: financial accounting and managerial accounting. **Financial accounting** focuses on preparing external financial statements that summarize past financial transactions. These historical financial statements are used to provide information to outside stakeholders like lenders, investors, and regulators.

Managerial accounting has an internal focus, providing information to help managers decide about operations and planning. Managerial accounting is more forward—looking, using budgets and forecasts. Understanding the difference between these two types of accounting helps managers know what information is relevant for particular business needs.

How do these two compare to real life?

Financial Accounting Example

At the end of the year, a rehabilitation clinic prepares a financial statement that shows $2 million in revenues and $1.8 million in expenses, resulting in $200,000 in net income. This historical financial statement summarizes the clinic's profitability over the past year and is prepared according to GAAP standards for external financial reporting.

GAAP stands for Generally Accepted Accounting Principles. Here's a quick explanation of GAAP:

GAAP is a set of standards and guidelines for financial accounting and reporting. It establishes proper accounting methods and reporting standards. The purpose of GAAP is to ensure consistent, transparent, and comparable financial statements between companies and across industries. It aims to establish standards of accountability, transparency, and accuracy in financial reporting. Following GAAP standards is mandatory for audited financial statements and public companies in the United States. Private companies may follow GAAP standards optionally.

Some key areas covered under GAAP include revenue recognition, asset valuation, accrual accounting, etc. Following GAAP means properly recording revenues when earned, expenses when incurred, as well as accurately reporting assets and liabilities. GAAP principles intend to reflect economic realities rather than just legal definitions. GAAP aims to provide more relevant and useful information for decision—making. While GAAP establishes standards, accountants must still apply professional judgment in some areas when applying GAAP principles. So there is some flexibility in interpretation.

Managerial Accounting Example

The rehabilitation clinic's manager wants to understand the profitability of the clinic's orthopedic department. She analyzes monthly revenue and cost data for the orthopedic department and finds that it generated $150,000 in net income over the past year. This analysis of the department's revenues and expenses is a managerial accounting approach focused on internal decision-making.

The manager also creates a budget for the orthopedic department for the upcoming year. She forecasts $200,000 in revenues and $170,000 in expenses, projecting $30,000 in net income for the department next year. This forward-looking budget exemplifies managerial accounting's focus on future planning and operational analysis, rather than past financial reporting.

Financial accounting creates historical financial statements for external use, while managerial accounting does internal analysis to aid in decision-making and planning for the future. The manager leverages managerial accounting approaches like departmental analysis and budgeting to gain insights beyond the finance department's annual financial statements.

Accrual vs. Cash Accounting

There are two types of accounting—*accrual and cash*—and we can use both, but they differ significantly in how they recognize revenue and expenses. Here's a breakdown of the key differences.

Accrual Accounting

Revenue Recognition: Revenue is recognized when *earned*, regardless of when payment is received. This means income is recorded when services are rendered, even if reimbursement hasn't happened yet.

Expense Recognition: Expenses are recognized when *incurred*, regardless of when payment is made. This means costs associated with providing services are recorded when they are incurred, even if payment hasn't been made to suppliers.

Benefits

- Provides a more accurate picture of an organization's financial performance over time by matching expenses incurred with the revenue earned.

- Useful for financial analysis and budgeting as it reflects economic activity more accurately.

- Required for publicly traded companies and some larger healthcare organizations.

Drawbacks

- Requires more complex accounting systems and tracking of receivables and payables.

- Can lead to fluctuations in income depending on the timing of payments and collections.

Cash Accounting

Revenue Recognition: Revenue is recognized when *payment is received*. This means income is only recorded when cash is actually collected from patients or insurers.

Expense Recognition: Expenses are recognized when *payment is made*. This means costs associated with providing services are recorded when bills are paid to suppliers.

Benefits

- Simpler to implement and manage as it only tracks actual cash inflows and outflows.

- Easier to understand and interpret for smaller healthcare organizations.

- Permitted for smaller businesses and some cash—based practices.

Drawbacks

- Doesn't provide a complete picture of an organization's financial performance as it doesn't reflect outstanding receivables and payables.

- Can distort profitability due to timing differences between service provision and payment.

- Less useful for financial analysis and planning.

How to Choose the Right Method

The accrual method is more conservative and, as mentioned, GAAP requires its use for hospitals. The choice between accrual and cash accounting depends on several factors.

- *Size and complexity of the organization*: Larger organizations with complex financial operations often choose accrual accounting for better insights.

- *Regulatory requirements*: Some industries or organizations may be required by law to use accrual accounting.

- *Financial reporting needs*: Accrual accounting offers more comprehensive information for analysis and reporting.

- *Internal control and management needs*: Tracking receivables and payables is crucial in accrual accounting for accurate financial management.

Ultimately, consulting with a qualified accountant can help you determine the most suitable accounting method for your specific needs and ensure compliance with relevant regulations.

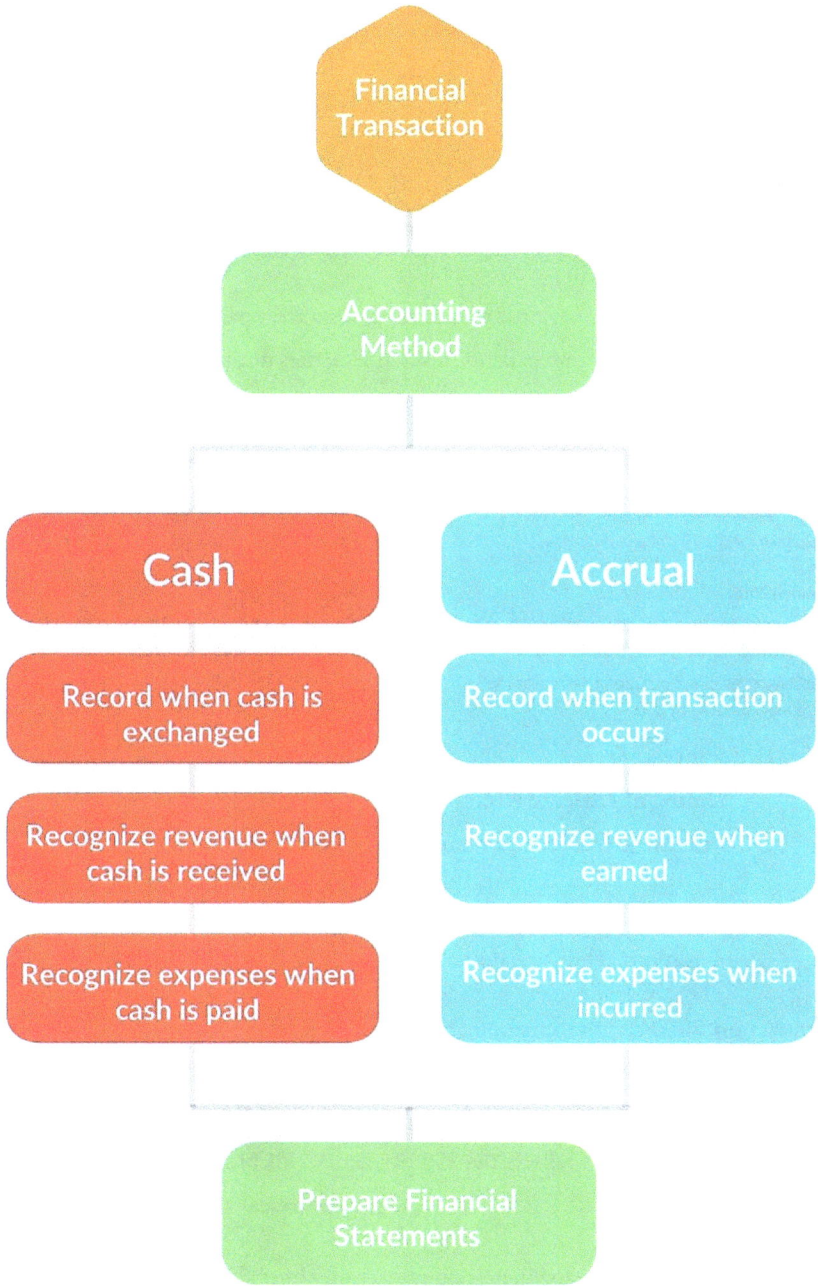

Figure 1. Comparison of Cash and Accrual Accounting Methods. Illustration of the fundamental differences between the cash and accrual accounting methods. Both methods lead to the preparation of financial statements, but the timing of transaction recognition differs.

Example

On 2/20/2024, the Rehab Department of a hospital orders a box of Theraband. The supplier delivers the box on 3/1/2024. The payment terms are net 30, meaning the department has 30 days to pay the supplier.

During March, we use the entire box of supplies to treat patients, but we will not receive reimbursement from patients' insurance carriers until April or May.

Accrual Accounting	Cash Accounting
February 20th:	**February 20th:**
Expense Recognition: The clinic records a $50 expense for the Theraband purchase.	No entry: Since the clinic hasn't paid for the Theraband yet, there's no impact on the accounting records.
March 20th:	**March 20th:**
Payment: The clinic pays the supplier $50 for the Theraband.	Expense Recognition & Payment: The clinic records a $50 expense for the Theraband purchase and simultaneously pay the supplier.
Accounts Payable: Accounting decreases the accounts payable by $50.	

Key Differences:

- **Timing of Expense Recognition:** Accrual recognizes the expense immediately when incurred, while cash recognizes it when paid.

- **Accounts Payable:** Accrual uses accounts payable to track outstanding obligations, while cash doesn't.

Impact on Financial Statements:

- **Accrual:** In February, the clinic's income statement shows a $50 expense, but your cash flow statement shows no cash outflow. In March, the cash flow statement reflects the $50 payment. This provides a more accurate picture of the clinic's financial activity over time.

- **Cash:** In February, there's no impact on either the income statement or cash flow statement. In March, both statements reflect the $50 expense and payment. This simplifies record—keeping but might not accurately portray the clinic's financial performance.

Key Financial Statements

Three essential financial statements summarize a rehabilitation practice's financial health. The balance sheet, income statement, and statement of cash flows are a company's core financial statements. Together, they provide a comprehensive overview of a company's financial performance.

Balance Sheet

A **balance sheet** is a financial statement that provides a snapshot of a company's financial position at a specific point in time. The balance sheet lists the company's assets, liabilities, and shareholders' equity as of a particular date. This typically includes the last day of a fiscal quarter or year.

- Assets are resources the company owns that have economic value. Common asset categories include cash, accounts receivable, inventory, property, and equipment.

- Liabilities are the company's financial obligations that have to be paid in the future. Common liabilities are accounts payable, wages payable, debt obligations.

- Shareholders' equity* represents the amount owners have invested plus any earnings the company retains. It's calculated as assets minus liabilities.

The balance sheet of a nonprofit healthcare company uses the term *Net Assets* instead of *Shareholders' Equity*, and it follows the restricted and unrestricted classifications specific to nonprofit accounting. This information gives insight into the use of donor funds. Here are a few key points:

- Since nonprofit companies do not have shareholders, the equity portion of the balance sheet has a different title.

- We divide Net Assets into categories based on donor restrictions.

- **Unrestricted net assets**—not subject to donor-imposed restrictions.

- **Temporarily restricted net assets**—subject to donor restrictions that actions of the company can fulfil or through passage of time.

- Organizations must hold funds classified as permanently restricted net assets indefinitely, with only the investment income accessible for use.

• The accounting equation for nonprofits is.

- *Assets = Liabilities + Net Assets*

The nonprofit uses unrestricted net assets for general operations and fringe benefits. Tracking changes in restricted vs. unrestricted net assets helps nonprofits demonstrate proper use of donor contributions. Lenders and donors may analyze net assets composition and trends to assess the financial health of a nonprofit healthcare company.

The balance sheet gets its name because it balances the company's assets against its liabilities plus shareholders' equity. The accounting equation that a balance sheet must adhere to is:

Assets = Liabilities + Shareholders' Equity

Analyzing the composition and trends of a company's balance sheet over time helps determine its financial health and liquidity. Comparing assets to liabilities shows its ability to pay obligations. The balance sheet provides a complementary overview of a company's finances along with other key statements, like the income statement and cash flow statement.

The balance sheet is a critical financial statement that summarizes a company's assets, liabilities, and shareholder equity at a specific point in time, following standard accounting rules and principles. It provides insight into the company's financial strength and position.

Some notes regarding the balance sheet:

• The balance sheet always *balances*.

- The accounting equation is:

  - *Assets – Liabilities = Shareholders' Equity*

- We need to move liabilities to the other side to make it a positive which gives us:

  - *Assets = Liabilities + Shareholders' Equity*

- The left side of this equation (Assets) represents the company or organizational resources; this is what we have, like cash.

- The right side of this equation (Liabilities + Equity) represents the sources of those resources; we use these resources to purchase assets.

SAMPLE BALANCE SHEET

Sample PT Clinic

Balance Sheet

April 1, 2024[1]

Assets[2]

Cash & Cash Equivalents	$25,000	
Accounts Receivable	$30,000	
Prepaid Expenses	$5,000	
Inventory (Supplies)	$2,000	
Total Current Assets		$62,000
Property & Equipment	$135,000[3]	
	- $15,000	
Less Accumulated Depreciation— Property & Equipment (net)	$120,000	
Furniture & Fixtures	$12,000	
	- $2,000	
Less Accumulated Depreciation— Furniture & Fixtures (net)	$10,000	
Vehicles	$9,500	
	- $1,500	
Less Accumulated Depreciation— Vehicles (net)	$8,000	
Goodwill	$50,000	
Total Non-Current Assets		*$188,000*
Total Assets		*$250,000*

Liabilities

Accounts Payable	$20,000	
Accrued Expenses	$10,000	
Unearned Revenue[4]	$5,000	
Total Current Liabilities		*$35,000*
Notes Payable	$75,000	
Total Non-Current Liabilities		*$75,000*
Total Liabilities		*$110,000*

Owner's Equity

Retained Earnings[5]	$140,000	
Total Equity		*$140,000*

Notes:

[1]Balance sheet is a single date.

[2]We should be able to liquidate current assets within a single year; non—current assets may take longer than that to liquidate, which is why we separate them.

[3]This is an offset calculation which means math is being done, no debit and credit column.

[4]Unearned or deferred means we've received cash, but have yet to do something with it; it's a liability until we use it.

[5]Retained earnings are the portion of a company's profit that we choose to keep back instead of distributing it to shareholders as dividends. Think of it as the company's "savings" accumulated over time.

Income Statement

An **income statement** is a financial statement that summarizes a company's revenues, expenses, and profitability over a specified period (typically quarterly and annually). People also call this report a profit-and-loss statement, statement of operations, or statement of earnings. It provides important insight into the financial health and performance of a business.

The key elements of an income statement are:

- **Revenue**—This refers to the money a company brings in from its business activities, such as sales of products or services. In our case, this is the revenue from patient care. This is further divided into gross patient service revenue and net patient service revenue. This category also includes other revenues, such as renting a room to another company.

- **Expenses**—These are costs incurred in the day-to-day operations of the business, such as wages, raw materials, advertising, etc.

- **Profit or loss**—This is the net income after subtracting total expenses from total revenue. Higher revenues and lower costs result in higher profitability.

- **Other income/expenses**—This includes other types of gains or losses like interest income or expenses.

The income statement shows a company's ability to generate profit by increasing revenues and managing costs and expenses. The format of this report is

$$Revenue - Expenses$$

Analyzing this report and these key elements over time can determine trends in profitability and compare performance across accounting periods or competitors.

SAMPLE INCOME STATEMENT

Sample PT Clinic

Income Statement

10/1/2022—9/30/2023[1]

Gross Patient Service Revenue[2]	750,000	
(Less) Contractual Adjustments		(400,000)
Net Patient Service Revenue	350,000	
Other Revenue		
Rent	12,000	
= Total Operating Revenue	**362,000**	
Operating Expenses		
Salaries and wages	120,000	
Supplies and materials	35,000	
Insurance Expense	5,000	
Rent	20,000	
Utilities	5,000	
Repair Expense	5,000	
Depreciation	10,000	
Interest Expense	5,000	
Bad Debt Expense	5,000	
= Total Operating Expenses	**210,000**	
Net Operating Revenue	**152,000**	
Non-Operating Revenue[3]	15,000	
Net Income	**167,000**	

Notes:

[1] Income Statements always have a date range.

[2] Most statements of operation begin with net revenue. But health care begins with GPSR to show how we get to NPSR (like contractual adjustments).

[3]Like interest payments from investments.

Statement of Cash Flows

While the income statement and balance sheet offer valuable insights, they don't directly tel' the story of 'ash flow. The **statement of cash flows** is a financial statement that summarizes the amount of cash and cash equivalents entering and leaving a company over a specified period. It measures how well a company generates cash to fund its operations and pay for investments. Unlike the income statement, which uses accrual accounting (recognizing revenue when earned and expenses when incurred), the statement of cash flows focuses on actual cash inflows and outflows and provides a clearer picture of your liquidity.

The statement of cash flows has three sections:

Cash flows from *operating* activities

Includes cash generated or spent from regular business operations and is an indicator of operating profitability. Inflows would include items like accounts receivable (A/R) and cash receipts. Outflows would include items like salaries, disbursing inventory, interest expenses, etc. This information isn't on statement of operations, so we need to regress the accrual data to cash data to get cash flow information.

Cash flows from *investing* activities

Includes cash used for investments, like purchasing fixed assets or investments. Inflows would include items like dividends and stock disbursements. Outflows would include things like the initial purchase of these assets.

Cash flows from *financing* activities

Includes cash from financing activities like borrowing or repaying loans, issuing stocks, and dividend payments. Inflows would include things like cash principle from the loan. Outflows would include things like interest payments on the debt.

Positive cash flow indicates the company has enough cash to fund operations and invest. Negative cash flow means it may need external financing to meet cash needs. The statement of cash flows complements the income statement and balance sheet. While income statements show *profitability*, cash flow statements show *liquidity*. Analyzing the statement of cash flows helps determine where a business's cash is coming from and going to. It provides insight into long-term viability.

This key financial statement gives investors and managers critical information about the company's cash inflows and outflows over a period. It helps evaluate financial and operating performance.

So why use both an income statement and a statement of cash flows?

When employing the accrual method of accounting, it is necessary to prepare a Statement of Cash Flows to monitor cash inflows and outflows. The statement of cash flows is used to disclose this previously undisclosed information. Cash flow information summarizes the major cash flows associated with the hospital's operations, financing, and investments. As a result, we are reverting to the cash accounting method for this statement.

SAMPLE STATEMENT OF CASH FLOWS
Sample PT Clinic
Operating (unrestricted) account
2023

Operating Activities

Service Fees Received	$500,000	
Insurance Reimbursements	$300,000	
Grant Funding	$25,000	
Equipment Purchases	($200,000)	
Rent and Utilities	($50,000)	
Salaries and Benefits	($400,000)	
Medical Supplies	($75,000)	
Net Cash Flow from Operating Activities		$100,000

Investing Activities

Sale of Equipment	$10,000	
Purchase of Land	($75,000)	
Net Cash Flow from Investing Activities		($65,000)

Financing Activities

Issuance of Debt	$150,000	
Loan Repayment	($50,000)	
Net Cash Flow from Financing Activities		$100,000
Net increase/decrease in cash		$135,000

Notes:

- This is a simplified example and may not reflect all relevant cash inflows and outflows for a rehab department/clinic.

- The specific categories and amounts will vary depending on the individual organization's operations, funding sources, and investment activities.

- It is important to consult with a qualified accountant to create an accurate and compliant statement of cash flows for your specific situation.

Remember, this is just a template to get you started. You'll need to fill in the specific details relevant to your rehab department or clinic to create a truly meaningful statement of cash flows.

Analyzing Financial Statements

Various analysis techniques can provide additional insights from the financial statements:

Horizontal and Vertical Analysis

Horizontal analysis looks at trends over time. Vertical analysis looks at percent composition.

Let's look at a company's income statement for two consecutive years for a horizontal analysis.

Income Statement

	2022	2023
Operating Revenue		
Gross Patient Service Revenue	600,000	750,000
Contractual Adjustments	400,000	500,000
Net Patient Service Revenue	200,000	250,000
Other Revenue		
Rent	12,000	12,000
Total Operating Revenue	212,000	262,000
Operating Expenses		
Salaries and wages	100,000	120,000
Supplies and materials	30,000	35,000
Rent and utilities	20,000	25,000
Total Operating Expenses	150,000	180,000
Net Operating Revenue	62,000	82,000
Non—Operating Revenue	10,000	15,000
Net Income	72,000	97,000

Horizontal analysis looks at the changes in line items year-over-year in two steps.

1. Calculate the dollar change:

   ○ Revenue: Increased by $50,000 ($262,000 – $212,000)

   ○ Expenses: Increased by $30,000 ($180,000 – $150,000)

   ○ Net Income: Increased by $25,000 ($97,000 – $72,000)

2. Calculate the percentage change:

   ○ Revenue: Increased by 23.6% [($50,000 ÷ $212,000) x 100]

○ Expenses: Increased by 20% [($30,000 ÷ $150,000) x 100]

○ Net Income: Increased by 34.7% [($20,000 ÷ $62,000) x 100]

This horizontal analysis shows that from Year 1 to 2, revenue grew by 23.6%, expenses by 20%, and net income by 34.7%.

Looking at dollar and percentage changes in financial statement lines over time highlights trends and growth rates that simple dollar amounts do not show on their own. This is the core purpose of horizontal analysis.

Let's now look at the same company's income statement for a single year for a vertical analysis.

DAVID POTACH

Income Statement

	2022	2023
Operating Revenue		
Gross Patient Service Revenue	600,000	750,000
Contractual Adjustments	400,000	500,000
Net Patient Service Revenue	200,000	250,000
Other Revenue		
Rent	12,000	12,000
Total Operating Revenue	212,000	262,000
Operating Expenses		
Salaries and wages	100,000	120,000
Supplies and materials	30,000	35,000
Rent and utilities	20,000	25,000
Total Operating Expenses	150,000	180,000
Net Operating Revenue	62,000	82,000
Non—Operating Revenue	10,000	15,000
Net Income	72,000	97,000

Revenue: $750,000

Contractual Allowance (Cost of Goods Sold): $500,000

Gross Profit: $250,000

Operating Expenses: $180,000

Net Income: $97,000

Vertical analysis looks at each line item as a percentage of a key figure, in this case revenue:

Contractual Allowance (Cost of Goods Sold) is **66.7%**

- $500,000 ÷ $750,000

Gross Profit is **33.3%**

- $250,000 ÷ $750,000

Operating Expenses is **24%**

- $180,000 ÷ $750,000

Net Income is **12.9%**

- $97,000 ÷ $750,000

Expressing the income statement accounts as a percentage of total revenue shows the composition and relative weight of each component. For instance, we can see the *Contractual Allowance*—also known as *Cost of Goods Sold*—makes up two-thirds of the total revenue, while Net Income is 12.9% of revenue.

Vertical analysis is useful for comparing percentages against historical averages for the company, competitor percentages, or industry benchmark percentages to evaluate financial performance.

The key difference from horizontal analysis is that vertical analysis looks at one period rather than changes across periods. It focuses on comparing proportions rather than dollar changes.

Benchmarking

Benchmarking involves comparing a company's key financial ratios or metrics to an industry standard or comparison point. This enables you to assess a company's performance compared to competitors, industry standards, or best practices. It is crucial for understanding financial performance, establishing improvement objectives, and identifying successful strategies. Comparing benchmarks helps with better strategic planning and decision making. Common benchmarks include:

- **Industry averages**—Compare to average ratios for the industry overall.

- **Direct competitors**—Compare to competitors in the same market segment.

- **Past performance**—Compare to the company's own historical ratios.

- **Best-in-class**—Compare to the top performers in that metric across an industry.

Ratios for benchmarking, such as profit margins, return on equity, accounts receivable turnover, inventory turnover, and other metrics, help identify strengths and weaknesses. If a company's ratios are below the benchmark, it may indicate problems or inefficiencies to address. Ratios above the benchmark imply stronger performance. Benchmarking works best when the benchmark is relevant and the time periods and calculation methods are consistent between the company and the benchmark. When used regularly, it helps to spot trends over time.

Liquidity

Liquidity refers to a company's ability to meet its short-term financial obligations and convert assets into cash. It measures how able a company is to pay off its current liabilities; in other words, it helps determine if the company has a strong short-term financial position or if there are signs of trouble on the horizon. Maintaining proper liquidity is vital for ongoing operations.

Key liquidity ratios include:

- **Current ratio**—Current assets divided by current liabilities. The current ratio measures the ability to cover short—term obligations.

- **Quick ratio**—Cash, marketable securities, and accounts receivable divided by current liabilities. The quick ratio measures the ability to meet obligations with most liquid assets.

- **Cash ratio**—Cash and cash equivalents divided by current liabilities. Cash ratio is the most conservative liquidity measure.

- **Working capital**—Current assets minus current liabilities. Working capital provides net liquid balance.

Higher ratios indicate greater liquidity and lower risk. Low liquidity means the company may struggle to pay expenses, suppliers, or short—term debt as they come due. Low liquidity also indicates potential cash flow issues. Benchmarking company liquidity over time and against industry averages helps spot improving or declining liquidity.

Here is an example of assessing liquidity ratios for a physical therapy practice:

Current Assets:

Cash—$50,000

Accounts Receivable—$100,000

Supplies—$10,000

Total Current Assets = $160,000

Current Liabilities:

Accounts Payable—$20,000

Accrued Expenses—$10,000

Debt Due in 12 Months—$50,000

Total Current Liabilities = $80,000

$$Current\ Ratio = \frac{Current\ Assets}{Current\ Liabilities}$$

$$= \frac{\$160,000}{\$80,000}$$

$$= 2.0$$

This current ratio of 2.0 means the practice has $2 in current assets for every $1 in current liabilities. This indicates strong short-term liquidity.

The practice could also calculate its quick ratio:

$Quick\ Assets = Cash + Accounts\ Receivable$

$\qquad = \$50,000 + \$100,000$

$\qquad = \$150,000$

$Quick\ Ratio = \dfrac{Quick\ Assets}{Accounts\ Receivable}$

$\qquad = \dfrac{\$150,000}{\$80,000}$

$\qquad = 1.875$

The high quick ratio further demonstrates this practice has strong liquidity to cover its short-term obligations.

While these ratios alone suggest that the practice has good financial liquidity, comparing these liquidity ratios to industry standards may lead to a different conclusion. According to industry data, average liquidity ratios for outpatient physical therapy practices are:

- Current Ratio: 3.1

- Quick Ratio: 2.7

Compare these benchmarks to our example practice's ratios:

- Current Ratio = 2.0

- Quick Ratio = 1.875

The practice's liquidity ratios are below industry average benchmarks.

While the practice still shows decent liquidity with ratios over 1.0, operating below industry averages could signal some vulnerability to covering short-term obligations. Some factors that may contribute to the lower liquidity:

- **High accounts receivable turnover days**—slow collection of A/R ties up liquidity.

- **Expensive equipment leases classified as current**—increases current liabilities.

- **Prepaying long-term debt due**—results in principal repayment obligations in next 12 months.

The practice should analyze its working capital cycle and cash conversion efficiency to understand what is causing the below average liquidity compared to peers. Boosting current assets through improved billing collections or restructuring some short-term debt may help strengthen the liquidity position closer to industry standards.

It is important to monitor liquidity over time and take corrective actions when trends are negative to match or exceed industry benchmark ratios. Having liquidity on par with competitors reduces financial risk.

Profitability

Profitability ratios measure a company's ability to generate income relative to revenue, assets, and equity. Higher profitability reflects better operational efficiency. Key profitability ratios include:

- **Gross profit margin**—Gross profit divided by revenue. Gross profit margin measures the profit after direct costs.

- **Operating profit margin**—Operating income divided by revenue. Operating profit margin looks at profit after operating expenses.

- **Net profit margin**—Net income divided by revenue. Net profit margin is the most comprehensive profitability measure.

- **Return on assets**—Net income divided by average total assets. Return on assets evaluates income generation from assets.

- **Return on equity**—Net income divided by average shareholders' equity. Return on equity measures return for shareholders.

We can compare these ratios over time to evaluate trends and against competitors or industry averages to benchmark performance. Higher ratios indicate greater efficiency in pricing and cost controls; declining ratios suggest potential problems. There are limitations to these comparisons as there are variations based on accounting methods; therefore, comparisons to past performance or similar companies are most meaningful.

Monitoring profitability ratios helps assess financial health and operational success. It identifies strengths or weaknesses in profit drivers and asset efficiency. This allows for actions to improve margins and returns.

Here is an example of profitability analysis:

A rehabilitation clinic has:

Revenue: $2,000,000

Total Expenses: $1,800,000

Cost of Goods Sold (COGS): $800,000

Net Income: $200,000

Average Total Assets: $1,000,000

Average Shareholder Equity: $500,000

$$Gross\ Profit\ Margin = \frac{Revenue - COGS}{Revenue}$$

$$= \frac{\$2,000,000 - \$800,000}{\$2,000,000}$$

$$= 60\%$$

$$Net\ Profit\ Margin = \frac{Net\ Income}{Revenue}$$

$$= \frac{\$200,000}{\$2,000,000}$$

$$= 10\%$$

$$Return\ on\ Assets = \frac{Net\ Income}{Average\ Total\ Assets}$$

$$= \frac{\$200,000}{\$1,000,000}$$

$$= 20\%$$

$$Return\ on\ Equity = \frac{Net\ Income}{Average\ Shareholder's\ Equity}$$

$$= \frac{\$200,000}{\$500,000}$$

$$= 40\%$$

This analysis shows the clinic has relatively strong profitability with gross and net margins of 60% and 10%. The high ROA and ROE demonstrate efficient use of assets and equity to generate income. The clinic can compare these ratios to its past performance, industry averages, or leading competitors to further evaluate its profit drivers.

Efficiency

Efficiency ratios measure how well a company uses its assets and manages its operations. Higher efficiency means the company is generating more revenue or value from its resources. Common efficiency ratios include:

- **Accounts receivable turnover**—Revenue divided by average accounts receivable (A/R). A/R measures how quickly A/R is collected. *Higher is better.*

- **Inventory turnover**—Cost of goods sold divided by average inventory. Inventory turnover measures how quickly inventory is sold. *Higher is better.*

- **Asset turnover**—Revenue divided by average total assets. Asset turnover measures revenue generated per dollar of assets. *Higher is better.*

- **Days sales outstanding**—Average accounts receivable divided by (Revenue/365). Days sales outstanding indicates average collection period for receivables. *Lower is better.*

These ratios help assess operational efficiency in managing inventory, collecting on receivables, and generating sales from assets. Comparing ratios to past trends or industry benchmarks identifies areas of improvement; for example, a lower A/R turnover could indicate problems with collections procedures. Limitations include variations in business models and accounting practices, so the focus should be on company or rehab—specific benchmarks. Analyzing efficiency supports better use of assets and working capital for improved financial performance.

Here are some examples of these key financial ratios:

Accounts Receivable Turnover

Revenue: $5,000,000

Average Accounts Receivable (A/R): $500,000

$$A/R \ Turnover = \frac{Revenue}{Average \ A/R}$$

$$= \frac{\$5,000,000}{\$500,000}$$

$$= 10x$$

This clinic collects its outstanding receivables 10 times per year on average. Higher turnover is better, indicating faster collection.

Inventory Turnover

Cost of Goods Sold (COGS): $1,000,000

Average Inventory: $100,000

$$Inventory \ Turnover = \frac{COGS}{Average \ Inventory}$$

$$= \frac{\$1,000,000}{\$100,000}$$

$$= 10x$$

This clinic turns over its rehabilitation supply and device inventory 10 times per year on average. Higher turnover indicates efficient inventory management.

Asset Turnover

Revenue: $5,000,000

Average Total Assets: $2,000,000

$$Asset \ Turnover = \frac{Revenue}{Average \ Assets}$$

$$= \frac{\$5,000,000}{\$2,000,000}$$

$$= 2.5x$$

This clinic generates 2.5x its average asset base in annual revenue. Higher asset turnover indicates assets are being used efficiently to generate revenues.

Days Sales Outstanding

Average Accounts Receivable: $500,000

Annual Revenue: $5,000,000

Days in Year: 365

$$Days\ Sales\ Outstanding = \frac{Average\ A/R}{(Annual\ Revenue \div Days)}$$

$$= \frac{\$500,000}{(\$5,000,000 \div 365\ days)}$$

$$= 36\ days$$

This clinic takes approximately 36 days on average to collect on its accounts receivable. Lower DSO is better, indicating shorter collection periods.

Debt Management

Debt management ratios measure a company's ability to meet its debt obligations and financial leverage position. Key debt ratios include:

- *Debt-to-equity ratio*—Total debt divided by total shareholders' equity. This shows the degree of financial leverage being used.

- *Debt ratio*—Total debt divided by total assets. This measures the percentage of assets financed through debt.

- *Times interest earned*—Earnings before interest and taxes (EBIT) divided by interest expense. Times interest earned indicates the cushion for meeting interest payments.

If we control costs and strategically use leverage, high debt levels do not necessarily indicate problems. However, an increasing debt burden signals potential trouble meeting obligations and higher bankruptcy risk. Conservative practices keep debt ratios and leverage under control, maintaining financial flexibility. Monitoring debt management helps ensure we can meet our obligations, while strategically using leverage to maximize opportunities. Keeping debt at sustainable levels supports financial stability.

Here are examples of these additional key financial ratios:

Debt-to-Equity Ratio

Total Debt: $2,000,000

Total Shareholders' Equity: $5,000,000

$$Debt\ to\ Equity\ Ratio = \frac{Total\ Debt}{Total\ Equity}$$

$$= \frac{\$2,000,000}{\$5,000,000}$$

$$= 0.4x$$

This clinic has a debt-to-equity ratio of 0.4x, meaning it has financed 40% of its assets through debt. Lower leverage is generally more favorable.

Debt Ratio

Total Debt: $2,000,000

Total Asset-: $10,000,000

$$Debt\ Ratio = \frac{Total\ Debt}{Total\ Assets}$$

$$= \frac{\$2,000,000}{\$10,000,000}$$

$$= 20\%$$

This clinic has a debt ratio of 20%, meaning it has financed 20% of its total assets through debt. Lower percentages are generally better.

Times Interest Earned

EBIT (Earnings Before Interest & Taxes): $1,000,000

Annual Interest Expense: $200,000

$$Times\ Interest\ Earned = \frac{EBIT}{Interest\ Expense}$$

$$= \frac{\$1,000,000}{\$200,000}$$

$$= 5x$$

This clinic has interest coverage of 5x, meaning its EBIT is 5 times its annual interest expense. Higher coverage indicates a greater ability to meet debt obligations.

Conclusion

Accounting is the language of business and provides quantitative insights to complement daily operations. Understanding these accounting principles and analysis techniques allows rehabilitation managers to better monitor the practice's financial health and make smart strategic decisions.

As Amanda wraps up her crash course in accounting with Brooklyn, she can't help but feel a sense of accomplishment. "Who knew that debits and credits could be so fascinating?" she muses, making a mental note to add "Master of the Balance Sheet" to her LinkedIn profile.

Personal Reflection: Amanda reflects on the importance of understanding the financial foundation of her department. She realizes that by mastering the basics of accounting, she can make more informed decisions, identify areas for improvement, and communicate more effectively with her financial colleagues. She commits to continuing her learning journey and to using her newfound knowledge to benefit her team and patients.

Chapter Two

Budgeting

Amanda's newfound confidence in accounting is put to the test when she's tasked with creating the department's annual budget. She stares at the blank spreadsheet, feeling like a deer in headlights. In a moment of desperation, she reaches out to one of her mentors, Dr. James Wilson, the CNO who's known for his budgeting prowess and his collection of quirky bow ties.

"Dr. Wilson, I need help! I'm supposed to create this budget, but I'm worried I'll end up accidentally funding a space mission instead of physical therapy," Amanda half-jokes.

Dr. Wilson chuckles, "Ah, the joys of budgeting! It's like trying to solve a Rubik's cube while juggling flaming batons. But don't worry, I've got some tricks up my sleeve."

With Dr. Wilson's guidance and a steady supply of caffeine, Amanda learns the art of projecting revenues, anticipating expenses, and creating a budget that balances patient care with financial responsibility. She even manages to sneak in a line item for a staff pizza party, because happy therapists make for better patient outcomes, right?

Creating financial budgets is a critical activity for managing and planning rehabilitation operations. Budgets estimate expected revenues, expenses, and capital needs over a future period. This chapter outlines types of budgets, budgeting methods, and analysis principles that rehabilitation leaders should understand.

Budgeting Types

When operating a rehabilitation business or department, budgets play a pivotal role in steering the organization toward its goals and ensuring financial stability. One of the key purposes of using budgets is to facilitate strategic decision making. By providing a comprehensive view of expected revenues, expenses, and investments, it empowers business leaders to align financial resources with organizational goals. It aids in determining the feasibility of proposed projects, assessing the need for external financing, and optimizing the allocation of resources to achieve long-term growth.

There are several types of budgets, but the text will focus on two, operating and capital. Each of these types of budgets serves distinct purposes, each contributing to the overall financial health and strategic decision making of a company.

Operating Budget

An **Operating Budget** is the cornerstone of day-to-day planning for rehab services. An operating budget forecasts an organization's revenues and expenses related to regular business operations over a specific period, usually for the upcoming fiscal year. Key elements of an operating budget typically include:

- **Revenue forecasts**—Projected income from services provided, government funding, grants, and fees.

- **Expense projections**—Expected costs for payroll, supplies, rent, utilities, and service delivery.

- **Operating profit estimate**—Revenues minus expenses shows projected operating income.

Forecasting patient or client volumes is crucial for projecting revenues and expenses in an operating budget, as volumes directly drive most budget line items. Accurately projecting volumes is critical for an operating budget that reflects realistic revenues, costs, and profits for a rehabilitation provider. Volume estimates help forecast revenue by multiplying the expected number of patients/visits by the average payment rate per visit provides the revenue projection. Knowing volumes allows us to align staffing needs to service the expected demand. In other words, projected patient volume determines the number of staff needed and the resulting payroll costs.

Volume forecasts guide supplies budget and facility expenses as well. Knowing expected patient volumes allows planning for required medical, therapy, or office supplies. Simply put, more patients require more supplies. Similarly, volume estimates affect facility expenses; higher volumes may require extended hours and higher utility, maintenance, and rental costs.

Ultimately, these volume projections impact profit margins as higher volumes can allow for fixed costs to be spread over more billable services, often improving profit margin. Changes in volume assumptions require re-forecasting, as shifts in volume projections cause updating corresponding revenues, expenses, and profits.

The operating budget is not static; it's a dynamic tool that we can adjust as market conditions change. Comparing actual performance against budgeted figures enables rehabilitation businesses to identify variances and adapt their strategies accordingly. This adaptability is crucial for maintaining financial resilience in the face of uncertainties.

Here is an example of an annual operating budget for a rehabilitation clinic:

Annual Operating Budget

Revenues:

Patient Service Revenue: $1,500,000

Government Funding: $200,000

Grants/Donations: $50,000

Total Revenues: $1,750,000

Expenses:

Staffing (including benefits): $900,000

Rent: $150,000

Equipment Leases: $100,000

Supplies: $200,000

Utilities: $50,000

Insurance: $75,000

Marketing: $25,000

Total Expenses: $1,500,000

$Operating\ Income = Revenues - Expenses$

$$= \$1,750,000 - \$1,500,000$$

$$= \$250,000$$

This budget forecasts expected revenues from services, government sources, and donations, along with itemized costs for payroll, facilities, materials, and other expenses. The result is $250,000 in operating income projected for the year.

Comparing actual financial results to this budget provides a tool to monitor operational performance and cash flows. The clinic can adjust the budget if revenues, expenses, or activity levels diverge significantly from the plan.

Operating budgets provide a blueprint for an organization's near-term operating activiti's and are essential for fiscal management, discipline, and strategic planning. This type of budget allows organizations to plan for upcoming resource needs and operating costs, align spending with organizational goals and priorities, and improve efficiency by minimizing unnecessary expenses. Operating budgets also support business growth by tying budgets to activity drivers while allowing a specific tool to monitor financial performance by comparing actual results to the budget.

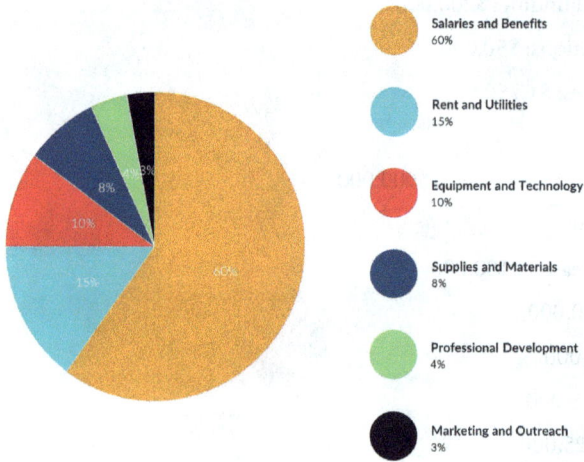

Rehab Department Annual Budget Breakdown. Distribution of a rehab department's annual budget across various expenditure categories.

Capital Budget

Unlike the operating budget, the **capital budget** focuses on major investments in assets that contribute to the company's growth and development. A capital budget deals specifically with major investment expenditures on assets, such as property, facilities, equipment, and technology. These are long-term investments that require large upfront costs but provide value over many years. The capital budget scrutinizes the potential returns on these investments, helping businesses allocate resources wisely to projects that promise long-term value and contribute to the company's overall prosperity.

Typical capital budget typically covers a time span of 3-10 years and includes items like:

- New facilities like buildings, land.

- Major equipment like imaging machines, therapy equipment.

- Information technology systems and infrastructure.

- Vehicles like vans and buses.

- Furniture and fixtures.

Steps for creating a capital budgeting include:

1. Generating proposals for capital investments and gathering estimates.

2. Analyzing payback period, ROI, NPV, and other criteria to evaluate proposals.

3. Prioritizing and selecting investments that align with strategic goals.

4. Determining capital financing sources—debt, equity, leases, and reserves.

5. Monitoring spending and performance of capital investments post-implementation.

Capital budgets require discipline to ensure investments maximize long-term returns and strategic value for the rehabilitation organization.

Here is an example 3-year capital budget for an outpatient rehabilitation clinic providing physical therapy, occupational therapy, and speech therapy services:

2023

- New Clinic Facility Construction—$2,000,000

- Physical Therapy Equipment—$50,000

- Patient Documentation System—$75,000

Total 2023 Expenditures = $2,000,000 + $50,000 + $75,000

= $2,125,000

2024

- Furnishings for New Clinic—$150,000

- Speech Therapy Assistive Devices—$25,000

- Wheelchair Accessible Van—$60,000

Total 2024 Expenditures = $150,000 + $25,000 + $60,000

   = $235,000

2025

- Occupational Therapy Equipment Upgrades—$30,000

- IT Network Infrastructure Refresh—$85,000

- Security Camera System—$20,000

Total 2025 Expenditures = $30,000 + $85,000 + $20,000

   = $135,000

Financing:
- Business Line of Credit—$1,500,000

- Lease Financing—$500,000

- Operating Cash Reserves—$500,000

This capital budget outlines major infrastructure investments planned over 3 years for the outpatient rehab clinic providing physical, occupational, and speech therapy. Comparing actual spending to the budgeted amounts will help control costs for these strategic projects.

Understanding the distinctions among these budget types is crucial for businesses to develop a comprehensive financial strategy. Operating and capital budgets collectively form a strategic framework, guiding organizations toward sustainable growth, financial resilience, and effective resource allocation. Matching expected revenues with required expenditures allows organizations to plan operations, manage costs, and allocate resources efficiently.

Budgeting Approaches

Several budgeting methods exist, each with advantages for different situations. This text will cover five of the most common, incremental, activity-based, value-based, zero-based, and flexible.

Incremental Budgeting

Incremental budgeting is an approach where we use the previous year's budget as a baseline and make *incremental* adjustments to arrive at the budget for the next period. It involves taking last year's actual figures and making modest changes based on expected needs for the upcoming period. For example, last year's spending on payroll was $50,000 per month. To create the new budget, we add a 5% increase to account for pay raises, resulting in a new payroll budget of $52,500. Small percentage increases or decreases apply to each budget category rather than developing the budget from zero.

This is one of the simplest and quickest budgeting methods. It requires minimal analysis of specific organizational needs and goals. A drawback is that it perpetuates previous periods' inefficiencies and does not account for activity changes or new initiatives. There is also a lack of big picture analysis. Incremental budgeting works best when there are no major strategy shifts planned and when we expect next year's activities to be very similar. It offers continuity from year-to-year. With incremental budgeting, rehabilitation managers should still assess if budget adjustments match strategic objectives for the period. Significant changes may require zero-based or flexible budgeting approaches.

Here is an example of incremental budgeting for a rehabilitation center's operating budget:

Revenue

Prior Year Actual: $1,500,000

Projected Increase: 3%

Budgeted Revenue = $1,500,000 × 1.03

= $1,545,000

Salaries

Prior Year Actual: $800,000

Projected Increase: 2%

Budgeted Salaries = $800,000 × 1.02

       = $816,000

Rent

Prior Year Actual: $60,000

No change

Budgeted Rent = $60,000

Supplies

Prior Year Actual: $100,000

Projected Increase: 5%

Budgeted Supplies = $100,000 × 1.05

       = $105,000

In this example, we incrementally adjust the major budget categories of revenue, salaries, rent, and supplies from the previous year's actual totals. The adjustments are based on basic percentage increases to account for expected changes in conditions. However, the rehabilitation center does minimal analysis on its specific activities and needs. This shows the simplicity but also limitations of incremental budgeting compared with zero-based or flexible approaches.

Activity-Based Budgeting

Activity-based budgeting involves developing budgets based on the specific *activities, services, and procedures* performed by an organization. It starts by estimating expected service volumes and workload drivers. For a rehabilitation facility, this could include a projected number of patient visits, procedures performed, therapy hours delivered, etc. The organization budgets for costs and staffing needs to match the service activity volumes. Higher projected volumes require more budgeted resources to handle the increased workload. Revenue projections align to the expected number of procedures billed or visits provided. When activity volume is the key cost driver, this approach provides more accurate budgets than incremental methods.

Activity-based budgeting works best in organizations where service levels fluctuate significantly. This method aligns staffing and materials to patient demand; if the rehabilitation provider plans major service expansions or reductions, an activity-based approach easily adjusts budgets accordingly based on the volume impacts. The challenge can be estimating volumes accurately. Incremental adjustments may still be required if projections are off. Overall, activity-based budgeting ties budgets directly to expected service levels, providing efficient allocation aligned to patient volumes.

Here is an example of activity-based budgeting using the same revenue, salaries, rent, and supplies categories:

Revenue

Projected Visits: 10,000

Average Revenue per Visit: $155

$Total\ Budgeted\ Revenue = 10,000 \times \$155$

$\qquad = \$1,550,000$

Salaries

Projected Visits: 10,000

Estimated Hours per Visit: 1

$Total\ Hours = 10,000 \times 1$

$\qquad = 10,000$

Salary Cost per Hour: $80

$Total\ Budgeted\ Salaries = 10,000 \times \$80$

$\qquad = \$800,000$

Rent

Projected Visits: 10,000

Rent Cost per Visit: $6

$Total\ Budgeted\ Rent = 10,000 \times \$6$

$\qquad = \$60,000$

Supplies

Projected Visits: 10,000

Supplies Cost per Visit: $11

Total Budgeted Supplies = 10,000 × $11

= $110,000

In contrast to incremental budgeting, this approach bases the revenue, salaries, rent, and supplies budgets on the projected visit volume rather than applying simple percentage increases. The activity driver of visits provides greater precision in aligning budgets to operating levels.

Value-Based Budgeting

Value proposition budgeting starts with identifying the desired *outcomes, impact, and value* an organization wants to achieve through their programs and services. Based on these goals, the organization develops budgets to fund the necessary resources for delivering the intended value and results. For example, a rehabilitation hospital may set a goal to achieve a 20% improvement in mobility for patients after knee replacement surgery. The budgets for staffing, equipment, and materials are determined based on what will be required to fund the programs to achieve that goal. This approach focuses budgets on funding the organizational priorities and initiatives that drive the most value. It starts with strategy rather than past spending levels.

Value proposition budgeting works best when there is clear strategic direction and strong metrics to measure outcomes. It aligns spending directly to impact. Challenges can include difficulty quantifying goals into budget line items and lack of performance data. Incremental adjustments may still be necessary. Overall, value proposition budgeting focuses budgets on providing the greatest value and impact. It ties spending to what matters most for rehabilitation organizations and their patients.

Outcomes-based budgeting is another term used to refer to value proposition budgeting. This term is sometimes used instead, but the core principles are the same. The focus is tying budgets directly to funding priorities that will drive the most value and impact, rather than basing it on previous spending alone. We quantify outcomes through metrics like lives improved, health status increased, quality of life enhanced, and align spending to improve organizational performance on those benefit metrics.

Here is an example of value-based budgeting compared to incremental and activity-based approaches:

Value-Based Budgeting

Organizational Goal: Improve patient mobility outcomes by 30%

Additional Physical Therapists Needed: 5 FTEs

Salary & Benefits per Therapist: $90,000

Total Additional Salary Cost = 5 × $90,000

    = $450,000

New Training Program: $25,000

Upgraded Therapy Equipment: $75,000

Total Budgeted Expenditures = $450,000 + $25,000 + $75,000

    = $550,000

In contrast to the previous examples, this approach starts with the organizational goal and then identifies and budgets the incremental resources needed to achieve that goal. The focus is funding priorities expected to drive the most value rather than starting from historical budgets.

Zero-Based Budgeting

Zero-based budgeting (ZBB) is an approach where budgets are *created from scratch* each new period regardless of past spending levels. Every expenditure must be newly justified based on current needs and priorities, rather than adjusting past budgets. With ZBB, the organization budgets from zero and analyzes and approves every function and expense instead of carrying them over. The benefits of ZBB include:

- Eliminates legacy inefficiencies by not carrying forward past waste.

- Enforces priority-based spending according to current conditions.

- Identifies cost savings through re-evaluation of needs.

Drawbacks can be the time required for comprehensive analysis and potential resistance from managers reluctant to re-justify budgets. ZBB is most useful when past waste or strategic changes necessitate an entirely new spending analysis. It is more complex than incremental budgeting. Many organizations use ZBB selectively for priority areas needing more discipline, while doing incremental budgets elsewhere. Overall, zero-based budgeting compels rigorous justification and alignment of budgets to organizational priorities on a regular basis. This can drive efficiency despite higher implementation effort.

Here is an example of zero-based budgeting for a rehabilitation center's operating budget:

Revenue

Expected Patients: 1,500

Average Revenue per Patient: $1,000

Total Budgeted Revenue = 1,500 × $1,000

$$= \$1,500,000$$

Salaries

Clinical Staff Needed: 10 FTEs

Support Staff Needed: 4 FTEs

Average Salary: $60,000

Total Budgeted Salaries = (10 × $60,000) + (4 × $60,000)

$$= \$600,000 + \$240,000$$
$$= \$840,000$$

Rent

Required Square Footage: 5,000 sq ft

Average Rent per Sq Ft: $20

Total Budgeted Rent = 5,000 × $20

$$= \$100,000$$

Supplies

Estimated Supplies per Patient: $75

Total Patients: 1,500

Total Budgeted Supplies = 1,500 × $75

= $112,500

Rather than incrementally adjusting historical budgets, zero-based budgeting analytically builds each budget category from a zero base according to specific needs. Every expenditure is fully re-justified each period. This example illustrates the rigor and priority alignment of zero-based budgeting.

Flexible Budgeting

Flexible budgeting creates multiple budget scenarios that can be *adapted* as business conditions change. This provides flexibility to respond to fluctuating activity levels. Traditional static budgets only work for one projected operating level. Flexible budgets adjust for different volume scenarios, like a range of patient visits. To build a flexible budget, we create static budgets for different possible activity levels (e.g. high, medium, low forecasts), and then tie revenue and expense line items to volume drivers and adjust them across each budget scenario. When actual volumes are higher or lower than initially projected, we apply the corresponding flexible budget scenario.

Benefits of flexible budgeting include the ability to respond rapidly to changing demand and support decision making amid uncertainties. Challenges include the additional upfront work developing multiple budgets and difficulty projecting volumes accurately. Tools like spreadsheet modeling help to create different budget models that are adjustable to a range of operating levels. Flexible budgets require some incremental calculations but provide greater adaptability for rehabilitation providers facing variable patient volumes and reimbursement levels.

Here is an example of flexible budgeting for a rehabilitation clinic:

Revenue

Volume Assumptions:

Low: 10,000 visits

Mid: 15,000 visits

High: 20,000 visits

Avg Revenue per Visit: $100

Low Volume Revenue = 10,000 × $100

          = $1,000,000

Mid Volume Revenue = 15,000 × $100

          = $1,500,000

High Volume Revenue = 20,000 × $100

          = $2,000,000

Salaries

Volume Assumptions:

Low: 10,000 visits

Mid: 15,000 visits

High: 20,000 visits

Avg Salary Cost per Visit: $50

Low Volume Salaries = 10,000 × $50

          = $500,000

Mid Volume Salaries = 15,000 × $50

          = $750,000

High Volume Salaries = 20,000 × $50

          = $1,000,000

This example shows revenue and salary budgets created for three different volume scenarios. Based on actual volume, the clinic selects the corresponding budget. This allows adapting to fluctuations in visits that a static budget would not accommodate.

Each type of budgeting has benefits and challenges. The best approach to budgeting depends on the rehabilitation provider's needs and culture while ensuring discipline and accountability.

Monitoring Performance

Once set, budgets provide performance benchmarks over the coming period. Regularly comparing actual results to the budget identifies variances. For example, actual labor costs exceeding budgeted amounts signals an issue needing correction.

There are several ways to evaluate how a clinic or department is performing compared to the budget. Here are some tips for calculating budget versus actuals regularly to monitor performance:

- Set a routine schedule for comparisons, such as monthly or quarterly. Monthly provides more frequent monitoring while quarterly reduces effort.

- Pull actual revenues and expenses from current financial statements for the period being analyzed.

- Compare actual amounts to the figures originally budgeted for that same time-frame.

- Calculate variances by subtracting actual from budget or calculate variance percentages.

$$\frac{Actual - Budget}{Budget}$$

- Analyze significant variances to understand what is driving them. Gather input from department heads or staff as needed.

- Identify if variances are onetime exceptions or indicate an ongoing issue. This will determine if budgets need adjusting.

- Investigate significant variances to determine root causes.

- Revise budget figures if business conditions have fundamentally changed. Update projections if needed.

- Keep variance analyses simple and focused on highlighting major issues and opportunities. Too much complexity loses value.

- Report key variances to management and present recommendations to get back on track or leverage opportunities.

- Take timely corrective action to address problems.

- Use technology like spreadsheets to automate variance calculations as much as possible for efficiency.

- Review performance against past periods to identify improvement trends.

Regular *budget versus actual* analyses, even if high-level, are crucial for monitoring organizational performance and financial health.

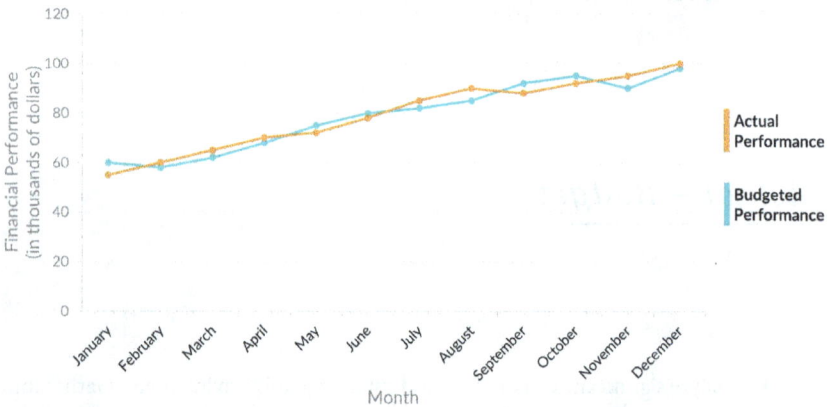

Figure 2b. Actual vs. Budgeted Financial Performance of Rehab Clinic. This line graph compares the actual and budgeted financial performance of a rehabilitation clinic over a 12-month period. The x-axis represents the months from January to December, while the y-axis shows the financial performance in thousands of dollars.

Actual vs. Budgeted Financial Performance of Rehab Clinic 2b

This line graph compares the actual and budgeted financial performance of a rehabilitation clinic over a 12-month period. The x-axis represents the months from January to December, while the y-axis shows the financial performance in thousands of dollars.

Conclusion

Budgeting provides a roadmap for rehabilitation providers' operational and 'financial goals. When paired with rigorous monitoring and analysis, it is a core tool for maintaining fiscal discipline and directing resources toward strategic priorities.

As Amanda puts the finishing touches on her department's budget, she can't help but feel a sense of pride. "I may not be ready to tackle world hunger just yet," she thinks, "but I can definitely conquer a spreadsheet or two."

Personal Reflection: Amanda realizes that budgeting is not just about numbers; it's about aligning resources with priorities and making tough decisions that impact patient care. She learns the importance of balancing financial responsibility with clinical excellence and commits to involving her team in the budgeting process to ensure a collaborative approach.

Chapter Three

Reimbursement Methods

Amanda's head is spinning faster than a centrifuge as she tries to make sense of the various reimbursement methods. She's pretty sure that "fee-for-service" isn't the same as "fee-fi-fo-fum," but she's determined to crack the code. In a meeting with the billing manager, Molly Johnson, Amanda unleashes her inner detective.

"Molly, I feel like I need a secret decoder ring to understand all these reimbursement codes," Amanda sighs, holding up a chart that looks like it belongs in a spy movie.

Molly grins, "Welcome to the wonderful world of healthcare reimbursement, where everything is an acronym, and the rules change faster than you can say 'ICD-10.'"

Together, they dive into the intricacies of Medicare, Medicaid, and commercial insurance, with Amanda occasionally wondering if it would be easier to just barter physical therapy for baked goods. But with Molly's guidance and a healthy dose of humor, Amanda starts to see the method behind the madness.

I n the United States, rehabilitation providers rely heavily on third—party reimbursement from public and private insurance plans. The reimbursement method used has significant implications for financial performance and incentives. Healthcare providers must understand how different reimbursement models impact revenues, costs, and profitability. As financial risk shifts to providers under bundled and capitated approaches, rigorous analytics and management of cost and quality become imperative. This chapter outlines the major reimbursement models, their incentives, and accounting considerations.

Fee-for-Service (FFS)

Fee-for-service pays providers for each service performed. The payment amounts can be determined based on costs, standard charges, or procedure schedules.

Cost-based FFS

Medicare uses cost-based FFS to cover allowable costs—like salaries, supplies, depreciation—of critical access hospitals (CAHs). Cost reports determine *per diem* payment rates and incentivize providing more services to cover fixed overhead costs. Cost settlements may recover additional costs or *claw back* excess payments.

Charge-based FFS

Charge-based FFS are common for private pay and self-pay patients. Provider sets charges for each service and patients are billed the full charge amount, but may negotiate discounts. Maximizing services performed is incentivized to increase total charges billed.

Private Pay

Contracted negotiated rates for private/commercial insurance are lower than full charges, but still FFS based on CPT and ICD codes. Pre-authorizations may be required. Providers have less collection risk. Volume incentives still exist.

Self-Pay

Providers set full charges and bill patients directly. Patients must pay but may negotiate discounts. Maximizing volumes and charges billed drives revenues. Providers must collect from patients.

Coding

Coding is crucial. Providers must code services accurately using CPT codes for procedures and ICD-10 codes for diagnoses to receive proper FFS reimbursement. Complete and specific coding documentation drives revenues.

CPT and ICD-10 Coding in Rehab Settings

In the world of rehabilitation, accurate and efficient coding is crucial for proper documentation, billing, and reimbursement. Two key coding systems play a vital role in this process: **Current Procedural Terminology (CPT)** and **ICD-10 (International Classification of Diseases, 10th Revision)**.

CPT Coding

- Focus: CPT codes define the specific services or procedures performed by healthcare professionals.

- Rehab Examples: CPT codes in rehab settings might include:

- 97110: Therapeutic exercise

- 97130: Gait training

- 97530: Manual therapy

- 97161: Physical Therapy Evaluation: Low Complexity

- Importance: Accurate CPT coding ensures proper billing for the specific services provided to patients.

- Selection: Selecting the most appropriate CPT code requires careful consideration of the specific procedure, duration, and complexity involved.

ICD-10 Coding

- Focus: ICD-10 codes classify diagnoses and medical conditions.

- Rehab Examples: ICD-10 codes in rehab settings might include:

  - G80: Cerebral palsy.

  - M19: Post-traumatic osteoarthritis.

  - S16: Fractures.

  - R41: Spinal cord injury.

- Importance: Accurate ICD-10 coding supports justification for services rendered, helps track health trends, and contributes to medical research.

- Selection: Choosing the most accurate ICD-10 code depends on the patient's primary and secondary diagnoses, contributing factors, and specific details of the condition.

Additional Considerations:

- Modifiers: We can use *modifiers* with CPT codes to provide additional details about the service performed, further enhancing accuracy.

- Staying Updated: Coding systems change periodically, so staying informed

> about updates and changes is essential.
>
> Chapter 4 provides further discussion and coverage of rehab coding.

Balance Billing

Balance Billing occurs when providers bill patients for the difference between charge-based rates and what insurance paid. This practice is strongly discouraged but may still be legal in some cases.

Fee For Service has many flavors but ultimately incentivizes volume over value. In other words, FFS models motivate providers to deliver a greater quantity of services in order to maximize their reimbursement amount. Payment is based on each discrete service rendered, not on quality or outcomes. This fragmentation and volume incentive has contributed to high costs and inefficiency in the US healthcare system.

Prospective Payment System

A **prospective payment system** sets a fixed reimbursement amount for a specific service beforehand, regardless of the actual cost or resources used. In other words, payments are based on predetermined rates per procedure or diagnosis unrelated to provider costs or charges. This approach to reimbursement still incentivizes volume but with an emphasis on constraining cost per service. Most settings, including inpatient, outpatient, home health, and skilled nursing facilities, use prospective payment systems.

Inpatient Prospective Payment System (IPPS)

Medicare's inpatient hospital PPS uses **Medicare Severity-Diagnosis Related Groups (MS-DRGs)** to classify admission into payment categories based on diagnoses, procedures, complications. **Inpatient hospital prospective payment system (IPPS)** is the PPS Medicare uses to pay hospitals for inpatient services under preset rates. Payments are determined by those DRGs which classify admissions based on diagnoses, procedures performed, complications, and other factors. Traditional CMS DRGs (created in the

1980s) had about 500 groups. Medicare Severity DRGs (MS-DRGs) were created in 2007 to better account for the severity of illness.

Despite being closely related, DRG and MS-DRG are not the same. Here's a breakdown of their differences.

DRG (Diagnosis-Related Group) is a general classification system that groups patients with similar diagnoses, treatments, and resource use. It's used by various healthcare payers, including private insurers and government programs besides Medicare.

MS-DRG is a specific type of DRG system specifically used by **Medicare**. It builds upon the general DRG system by *adding a severity level* based on factors like complications, comorbidities, and patient's functional status. This allows for *more accurate reimbursement* based on the actual complexity of the case.

In simpler terms, MS-DRG is a more specific and refined version of the DRG system, tailored for the unique needs of the Medicare program. The key differences between traditional DRGs vs MS-DRGs are:

- MS-DRGs expanded the number of groups to over 700 to improve clinical specificity.

- MS-DRGs splits DRGs based on presence of complications/comorbidities (CC) and major complications/comorbidities (MCC) to adjust for severity.

- MS-DRGs are further adjusted for factors like age, discharge status, and length of stay.

- MS-DRGs provide greater reimbursement accuracy and incentives to treat more complex patients.

IPPS uses MS-DRGs to enhance the original DRG model to better classify inpatient hospital admissions to determine how much Medicare pays the hospital for that stay regardless of its actual costs.

Outpatient Prospective Payment System (OPPS)

OPPS is the system Medicare uses to pay for hospital outpatient services. It uses **Ambulatory Payment Classifications (APCs)** to categorize services into groups for standardized payments. When a hospital provides an outpatient service, it is assigned an APC with a relative weight that is multiplied by a conversion factor to determine payment. OPPS aims to pay for the procedures and services provided, rather than simply reimbursing costs. Services covered under OPPS include emergency department visits, clinic visits, same-day surgeries, lab tests, therapies, imaging, drugs, medical supplies, and preventive services. OPPS provides a packaged payment that bundles costs for the primary procedure along with supportive services like supplies, equipment, drugs. Medicare updates OPPS payment rates and APC classifications annually based on the latest cost data and incentivizes hospitals to manage their outpatient costs below the fixed prospective rates set by Medicare for each APC. Compliance with proper OPPS billing, coding, and documentation procedures is essential to getting reimbursed accurately.

Ambulatory Payment Classification

Outpatient PPS uses APC groups to pay for outpatient procedures and services based on CPT codes. APCs are the payment categories Medicare uses to reimburse hospitals for outpatient services under OPPS. Services are grouped into APCs based on clinical similarity and resource usage. Each APC has an assigned relative weight. When a hospital provides an outpatient service, it is assigned to an APC group with a corresponding relative weight. The relative weight is multiplied by a conversion factor dollar amount to determine the final payment rate for that service. There are over 700 APC groups covering medical procedures, imaging, lab tests, therapy services, and other outpatient hospital services.

APC examples include Cardiac Valve Replacement APC, Level 2 Excision/Biopsy APC, and Physical Therapy APC. The APC grouping determines the payment hospitals receive for each outpatient service, providing an incentive to manage costs within each group. CMS updates the APC groups, relative weights, and conversion factor annually.

Home Health PPS

The **Home Health Prospective Payment System (HH PPS)** is a payment system used by Medicare to reimburse home health agencies (HHAs) for providing services to patients in their homes. Like the IPPS and OPPS, it is a prospective payment system, meaning Medicare pays a fixed amount for an episode of care based on a predetermined classification of the patient's needs, regardless of the actual cost of providing the services. The unit of payment is a **60-day episode of care**. This means Medicare pays a single, bundled payment for services provided during this period.

The payment is divided into two parts.

- *Initial Payment*: This is paid upfront based on the patient's condition at the beginning of care.

- *Final Payment*: This is paid after the episode ends and is adjusted based on any changes in the patient's condition or additional services provided.

The HH PPS uses a system called **Home Health Resource Groups (HHRGs)** to classify patients into categories based on their diagnosis, functional limitations, and therapy needs. Different HHRGs receive different payment rates. The goal of the HH PPS is to control Medicare spending by setting fixed payment rates. It also encourages efficiency by incentivizing HHAs to deliver services in a cost-effective way while also promoting quality care by setting performance standards for HHAs.

The HH PPS has been in place since 2000 and has undergone several revisions over the years. The latest version, implemented in 2020, introduced significant changes, including:

- *Case mix adjustment:* Increased emphasis on patient complexity and functional limitations in determining payment rates.

- *National standardized payment rates:* Eliminating regional variations in payment rates.

- *Outlier payments:* Additional payments for cases with unusually high costs.

Skilled Nursing Facility PPS

Skilled Nursing Facility Prospective Payment System (SNF PPS) is a system used by Medicare to reimburse SNFs for the care provided to patients. Similar to the other PPS versions described, the SNF PPS is a prospective payment system. The unit of payment is a *per diem* **rate**, which means the SNF receives a fixed amount per day for each Medicare patient they care for; the *per diem* rate is adjusted based on the patient's **case mix index (CMI).**

- *Diagnosis:* The primary and secondary diagnoses of the patient.

- *Functional limitations:* The patient's level of independence in performing daily activities (ADLs).

- *Comorbidities:* The presence of additional medical conditions.

- *Therapy needs:* The type and intensity of therapy services required.

Patients with higher needs and complexity generally receive higher *per diem* rates.

Unlike the HH PPS, the SNF PPS is a single payment covering all Medicare-covered services, including nursing care, therapy services, room and board, meals, and medical supplies. To determine the appropriate case mix and payment level, SNFs are required to conduct regular assessments on their patients. These assessments typically occur upon admission, around days 5, 14, 30, 60, and 90 of the stay, and additionally whenever the patient's condition significantly changes.

The SNF PPS aims to control Medicare spending by setting fixed payment rates. It also has a goal of improving resource allocation by allocating more resources to patients with higher needs. Like the other PPS covered, the promotion of quality care is achieved by linking payments to patient assessments and outcomes.

> In the context of the case mix index (CMI), a higher number signifies more complex and resource—intensive patients. This is because the CMI considers various factors that contribute to patient complexity, such as:
> - Severity of diagnoses
>
> - Comorbidities (presence of additional medical conditions)

- Functional limitations

- Therapy needs

By calculating the average weighted complexity of all patients treated at a facility, the CMI provides a single measure to compare and analyze the resource utilization across healthcare facilities. This metric plays a crucial role in:

- *Reimbursement*: Hospitals and other healthcare facilities with higher CMIs generally receive higher reimbursement rates from insurance companies and government programs, as they are deemed to be caring for more complex patients requiring more resources.

- *Performance benchmarking*: Comparing CMIs allows for comparison of case complexity across different facilities, helping assess their efficiency and resource allocation.

- *Strategic planning*: Understanding the CMI can help healthcare organizations plan their resources and service offerings based on the prevalent patient needs in their service area.

Therefore, a higher CMI indicates a more complex patient population, which translates to increased resource utilization and potentially higher reimbursement rates within the healthcare system.

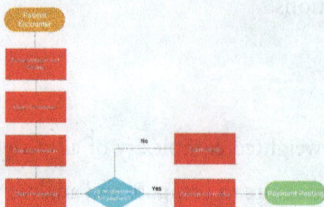

Figure 3a. Reimbursement Flow Under a Prospective Payment System. Key steps involved in the reimbursement process under a prospective payment system (PPS) for rehabilitation services.

Bundling

Bundling combines payments for all providers and services involved in an episode of care into one lump sum amount. This incentivizes coordination and resource efficiency across the care continuum. Providers share cost savings achieved. Bundling is growing but still limited in use. All the services needed during an episode (e.g., surgery, hospital stay, follow-up) are bundled together. Providers split the bundled payment amount based on the services they delivered.

There are several types of bundles, depending on the setting, including:

- Inpatient stays involving multiple providers.

- Outpatient episodes around procedures.

- Post-acute care pathways.

The goals of bundling are to reward coordination and continuity across care settings, align provider incentives around value and outcomes, reduce excessive services and costs, and enable providers to share in cost savings. Bundled models require coordination between physicians, hospitals, post-acute facilities to provide efficient care within the set payment amount. This approach then allows participants to split gains and risks, encouraging teamwork. This model is still limited but growing as Medicare expands programs like BPCI Advanced and CJR.

The Total Joint Replacement Bundle includes all services around a knee or hip replacement surgery episode. Providers included in bundle:
- Orthopedic surgeon

- Hospital facility fees

- Post-acute care facility fees

- Outpatient physical therapy

The total bundled payment amount is based on the expected average costs for a joint replacement episode. Providers coordinate to deliver care within the set bundle amount; if actual costs are lower than the bundled rate, providers share the savings. This should encourage physical and occupational therapists to maximize outcomes while constraining unnecessary costs. The bundle spans the entire care journey, aligning incentives around long-term results rather than individual volumes.

Capitation

With **capitation**, providers receive a fixed prepayment amount per patient per month or per member per month (PMPM) to cover all necessary services. Incentives shift radically towards preventive care, reducing unnecessary services, and keeping patients healthy. Capitation transfers the financial risk from payers to providers.

Regardless of how much or how little care each patient actually receives, the PMPM payment remains fixed. Capitation covers a defined patient population over a set time-frame (typically 1 year). Providers assume full financial risk—they must manage within the capitation budget to avoid losses. The benefits of a capitation model are:

- Focus on preventive care and health maintenance to reduce expensive illnesses.

- Conservative use of only essential services to avoid overspending the capitation budget.

- Tight care coordination and management of high-need patients.

Capitated models require advanced analytics on utilization patterns and patient risk to set accurate PMPM rates. Partial capitation for certain services is also common. Upside and downside risk models are used to share risk. Overall, capitation fundamentally shifts incentives toward keeping a population as healthy as possible long-term rather than utilization volume. Managing care delivery within the capitated budget is critical.

Feature	Fee For Service (FFS)	Bundled Payments	Capitation
Payment Basis	Payment for each individual service provided	Single payment for all services related to a specific condition or episode of care	Fixed payment per patient per month, regardless of services provided
Financial Risk for Provider	Low risk; provider is paid for each service rendered	Moderate risk; provider is responsible for managing costs within the bundled payment	High risk; provider is responsible for all patient care costs within the fixed payment
Incentives for Providers	Encourages volume and complexity of services	Encourages efficiency and care coordination within the episode of care	Encourages preventive care and cost control
Quality of Care Focus	Limited incentives for quality improvement	Encourages quality to avoid complications and readmissions within the episode	Encourages a focus on overall patient health and outcomes
Care Coordination	Minimal incentives for care coordination across providers	Encourages coordination among providers involved in the episode of care	Encourages coordination across all aspects of a patient's care
Administrative Complexity	High complexity due to billing for each service	Moderate complexity; requires defining and managing episodes of care	Low complexity; a single payment covers all services
Patient Cost-Sharing	Patients may have copayments or coinsurance for each service	Patients may have a single copayment or coinsurance for the entire episode	Patients typically have minimal cost sharing, often through a monthly premium
Provider Revenue Potential	High revenue potential based on volume and complexity of services	Moderate revenue potential; opportunity for shared savings if costs are managed effectively	Low revenue potential; fixed payment per patient regardless of services provided
Examples in Rehabilitation	Therapy sessions, evaluations, modalities billed separately	Bundled payment for post-acute care following a joint replacement	Capitated payment for all outpatient therapy services for a patient population

Figure 3b. Comparison of Key Features Across Reimbursement Models. Side-by-side comparison of the key features of fee-for-service, bundled payments, and capitation reimbursement models.

Concierge medicine, also known as boutique or retainer medicine, is a healthcare model in which patients pay a membership or retainer fee to access enhanced and personalized care. This model of rehabilitation delivery, while not common, is increasing in popularity. Capitation and concierge medicine share some similarities but have some important differences.

Similarities

- Both involve paying a fixed periodic fee for services.

- In both models, patients pay upfront for care rather than fees for each service.

Differences

- **Scope**—Capitation covers all necessary healthcare services while concierge medicine focuses primarily on enhanced primary care access and services.

- **Risk**—In capitation, providers take on full financial risk for managing within the set payments to cover comprehensive care. Concierge care has lower financial risk for providers.

- **Size**—Capitation arrangements cover large groups of patients. Concierge care is typically for individuals or smaller practices.

- **Access**—Capitation doesn't necessarily improve access compared to insurance models. Concierge care offers improved access through lower patient panels and amenities.

- **Cost**—Capitation aims to reduce unnecessary costs through tight utilization management. Concierge fees are generally higher for expanded services.

In essence, capitation is a large-scale insurance payment model, while concierge is a boutique care model. The provider's incentives differ substantially.

Insurance Programs

Most rehab settings continue to rely on third parties—usually health insurance companies—to pay for most rehab services. Here is an overview of major insurance programs and how they affect rehabilitation services:

Medicare

Medicare covers medically necessary rehab services under Part A and B and primarily uses prospectively set fee schedules with some bundled payments. Medicare requires copays and deductibles and uses controls aimed at reducing unnecessary services. Private insurance companies offer Medicare Part C (Medicare Advantage) and provide an alternative way to receive Medicare benefits, often featuring additional coverage like vision and dental. Medicare Part D does not involve rehab services; this is optional prescription drug coverage offered by private insurance companies to help cover the cost of medications for Medicare beneficiaries.

Medicaid

Medicaid is a joint federal-state program that provides health insurance coverage for low-income individuals and families. In each state, Medicaid uses various models, such as FFS, PPS, and capitation. Medicaid covers rehab services mandated by each state's program and each state reimburses in unique ways through FFS, managed care, or administration contracts. Medicaid typically has lower payment rates than Medicare or private insurance.

Private Insurance

Private insurers usually negotiate different payment structures—like FFS or capitation—based on market competition and their risk tolerance. Network access also plays a significant role with these markets. Not all insurance plans pay with the same model; there are three primary variations.

Health Maintenance Organizations (HMOs)

Patients are restricted to a limited network of providers, typically requiring referrals from a primary care physician to access rehab services. This limits out-of-network coverage and allows the HMO to control rehab utilization to manage costs.

Preferred Provider Organizations (PPOs)

Patients have greater flexibility in choosing providers, including those outside the network. However, out-of-network services come with higher deductibles and copays compared to in-network options. This approach gives patients more choice but offers less control over costs for the insurer compared to HMOs.

Point-of-Service (POS)

These plans offer a hybrid approach, allowing patients to use an HMO-like network for lower costs or access out-of-network providers with greater flexibility, similar to PPOs, but at higher cost-sharing levels.

Cash-Based Clinics

In contrast to the traditional model, where insurance companies cover or heavily influence physical therapy treatments, **cash-based clinics** take a different approach. Cash-Based clinics require patients to pay the therapist directly for services, bypassing insurance companies. Therapists set their own prices and treatment plans, independent of insurance limitations. This approach allows for more freedom and flexibility in designing therapy programs.

This is a very attractive model for many. It has the potential to allow more *patient-centered care*. Therapists can focus on individual needs and goals without restrictions imposed by insurance companies, which can lead to more personalized and effective treatment plans. Because patients don't need to wait for insurance approvals, *treatment may begin sooner*. Therapists can use a wider range of techniques and technologies that *insurance may not cover*. There is also *improved communication and transparency*; patients pay directly, so they clearly understand the costs and services involved.

Perhaps the biggest downside is the cost. Cash-based rehab *can be more expensive* than insurance-covered therapy, as not everyone can afford the upfront costs of cash-based services. Obviously, cash is used to cover services, not insurance companies; this means patients potentially miss out on using their insurance benefits of therapy.

Which patients might benefit the most from cash-based clinics? There are conditions with limited insurance coverage. Examples of these include:

- *Neurological conditions*: Stroke, spinal cord injuries, and chronic pain often require long-term, individualized therapy that insurance may not fully cover. Cash-based models allow therapists to provide comprehensive treatment plans without limitations.

- *Musculoskeletal conditions*: Repetitive strain injuries, chronic pain syndromes, and post-surgical rehab sometimes face limitations or coverage gaps with insurance. Cash-based PT offers greater flexibility to address these specific needs.

- *Pelvic floor dysfunction*: Issues like incontinence or sexual dysfunction can be sensitive and require specialized PT approaches that traditional insurance may not cover. Cash-based models allow for discreet and personalized treatment options.

- Individuals seeking *specialized or advanced treatments*, like:

  - **Athletes requiring performance optimization**: Cash-based therapists can tailor programs to specific sports or performance goals, using techniques not always covered by insurance.

  - **Postpartum/prenatal care**: Specialized support for recovery after childbirth or preparation for pregnancy may not be fully covered by insurance. Cash-based programs can offer additional personalized attention and services.

○ **Wellness and preventative care**: Proactive physical therapy for injury prevention or general fitness can prove expensive or get excluded from insurance plans. Cash-based models allow individuals to invest in preventative care directly.

• Patients prioritizing *specific benefits*.

○ **Faster access to care**: Cash-based models typically eliminate the need for pre-authorizations and referrals, leading to quicker treatment start times.

○ **Personalized and flexible treatment plans**: Therapists can design programs tailored to individual needs and goals, without restrictions imposed by insurance companies.

○ **Improved communication and transparency**: Direct payment fosters stronger relationships between patients and therapists, leading to open communication and shared decision-making.

Cash-based physical therapy offers an alternative to the traditional model, providing greater freedom and flexibility for both patients and therapists. While it comes with cost considerations, it can be a suitable option for individuals seeking personalized and efficient care, particularly when insurance coverage is limited.

Conclusion

Navigating this patchwork of reimbursement models requires rehabilitation providers to analyze financial incentives and adjust operations accordingly, so close analysis of payer mix and contract terms is essential. Understanding the opportunities and risks posed by different payment systems is vital for financial planning and sustainability.

As Amanda and Molly wrap up their reimbursement crash course, she can't help but snicker. "I never thought I'd be so excited about acronyms," she smiles, "but here we are, ready to take on the world—as you said—one ICD-10 code at a time."

Personal Reflection: Amanda reflects on the complexity of the healthcare reimbursement landscape and the importance of staying informed about changes and trends. She realizes that by understanding the intricacies of different payment models, she can optimize her department's revenue and ensure the sustainability of their services. She commits to ongoing education and collaboration with her billing team to navigate the ever-changing world of reimbursement.

Chapter Four

Productivity

Amanda's on a mission to boost productivity in the department, armed with a stopwatch and a determination to make every minute count. She's pretty sure that "productivity" isn't just about how many post-it notes she can stick on her forehead, but she's ready to learn. In a meeting with the inpatient supervisor, Ella Chen, Amanda prepares to unleash her inner efficiency guru.

"Ella, I've been analyzing our productivity data, and I think we might squeeze in a few more patient visits if we cut back on the water cooler gossip sessions," Amanda jokes, holding up a chart that looks like a connect-the-dots puzzle.

Ella laughs, "Well, I'm all for efficiency, but let's not forget the importance of a well-hydrated staff! In all seriousness, though, there are some strategies we can implement to help our therapists work smarter, not harder."

Together, they brainstorm ways to streamline documentation, optimize scheduling, and create a culture of continuous improvement. Amanda even suggests a friendly competition to see who can come up with the most creative productivity hack, with the prize being a coveted "Employee of the Month" parking spot.

P roductivity is a multifaceted concept with several nuances, interpretations, and definitions. It is a vital metric in healthcare for evaluating operational efficiency and financial performance at both system and clinician levels. For this book, productivity is the efficiency in producing something. This is the most common definition, focusing on getting things done and doing them with minimal waste of time, resources, or effort. This chapter covers key productivity measures used in managing healthcare and rehabilitation services. The goal of measuring productivity at multiple levels is to create effective systems that support our goals while supporting our individual contributions and well-being. To understand productivity and how to measure it clearly, establishing definitions for both revenue and expenses is crucial, as they both contribute to productivity metrics.

Revenue

Revenue in healthcare is the amount of money generated by a healthcare organization or provider through patient care, services, and operations over a certain period of time. Healthcare organizations or providers earn revenue by charging and collecting payments from patients, insurance companies, government programs, or other payers for the medical services they provide. For rehab departments and clinics, the most common source of revenue is **patient service revenue;** patient service revenue includes payments for clinical services provided to patients. Other sources of revenue in rehab settings include sales of equipment or supplies, rental of unused space, and contracts with companies or schools.

Those working in a hospital setting may also see the following revenue sources:

- **Grants/Donations**—Funds received from government grants, philanthropic gifts, fundraising campaigns.

- **Non-patient care revenue**—Examples include cafeteria sales, gift shops, parking.

- **Investment/interest income**—From investments, endowments, and cash reserves.

- **Educational revenue**—Payments related to education programs, research.

In rehabilitation settings, there are three important types of patient service revenue: Gross Patient Service Revenue (GPSR), Net Patient Service Revenue (NPSR), and collected revenue.

Gross Patient Service Revenue (GPSR) refers to the total charges or list prices billed for rehabilitation services provided before any reductions, contractual allowances, or adjustments. **Net Patient Service Revenue (NPSR)** is the actual revenue received and recorded after subtracting discounts, allowances, and any other reconciling adjustments from the initial gross charges. **Collected revenue** is the actual payment amounts received and can be recognized as revenue after providing services to patients.

GPSR reflects total billed charges and does not account for contractual adjustments by payers; while NPSR shows the net revenue after these. GPSR is higher and represents potential revenue. NPSR is lower and shows actual revenue. Tracking both helps rehabilitation providers analyze charge capture, reimbursement realization rates, revenue cycle effectiveness, and actual profitability. Monitoring metrics like NPSR as a percentage of GPSR identifies opportunities to improve collections and minimize wasted charges or underpayments.

Here is an example showing how analyzing Net Patient Service Revenue (NPSR) as a percentage of Gross Patient Service Revenue (GPSR) can provide insights into potential revenue improvements.

A rehabilitation clinic has the following annual revenue:

Gross charges: $1,000,000

Contractual adjustments: $200,000

Net Patient Service Revenue: $800,000

$$NPSR \ as \ a \ percentage \ of \ GPSR = \frac{NPSR}{GPSR} \times 100$$

$$= \frac{\$800,000}{\$1,000,000} \times 100$$

$$= 80\%$$

This shows the clinic is collecting 80% of its gross charges as net revenue after payer adjustments. The 20% contractual adjustment rate seems in line with typical managed care contracts. But if the rate is higher than benchmarks or past years, it may indicate issues negotiating with payers or improper discounting. Commercial plans would typically have a higher percentage (maybe 85%) compared to Medicare or Medicaid plans (perhaps 70%) based on reimbursement levels. Thus, if the clinic's Medicare percentage is lower than benchmarks, there could be opportunities to capture more revenue through improved coding/documentation. The clinic should analyze the metric by payer and service line to identify any billing, documentation or contracting issues limiting NPSR. Making improvements to achieve a higher NPSR percentage of GPSR ensures the clinic maximizes reimbursement and revenue collection from its gross charges.

Expenses

Expenses in healthcare cover the costs of delivering patient care and operating facilities and systems. These costs include things like labor, supplies, facilities, technology, and administration. While "cost" has a broader business management context and "expenses" has a more specific accounting definition, we will use the two terms interchangeably to refer to the costs of operating and delivering patient care services.

Fixed vs. Variable Costs

We can break down expenses into fixed and variable categories. **Fixed costs** are expenses that remain constant regardless of volume or activity level. For example, a major medical equipment purchase incurs a *fixed* cost that remains the same whether a healthcare provider sees 100 or 1,000 patients per month.

Other fixed costs like rent, salaries, and utility bills also stay static in total even as service volumes fluctuate. As service volumes increase, the fixed costs per unit of service decrease because the total fixed amount is spread over more patients.

Fixed costs for a rehab department include:

- **Salaries of staff physical therapists**—Most organizations fix the total compensation of staff therapists annually, regardless of patient volume. This is typically the largest expense.

- **Rent for the clinic space**—The clinic space has a set monthly cost for rent, regardless of how many patients staff therapists treat.

- **Utilities like electricity and Wi-Fi**—Contracted base costs unaffected by volume fluctuations.

- **Equipment leases**—Fixed regular lease payments for items like treadmills.

Variable costs are expenses that change in direct proportion to the volume of services. The more patients treated, the higher the variable costs. Examples are therapy supplies and hourly clinician wages. If patient volume doubles, variable costs double.

Variable rehab costs that change based on patient volume include:

- **Supplies used**—More patients means more supplies consumed.

- **Patient appointment hourly wage staff**—Only paid for hours worked with patients.

- **Therapy equipment maintenance**—Increases with higher equipment usage.

- **Patient documentation software per-encounter fees**—Rise with more patient visits.

Careful management and control of expenses is crucial for healthcare organizations to maintain positive margins. Driving down "cost per unit of service" is a frequent goal to improve profitability. Common strategies involve labor productivity, supply chain efficiencies, and care standardization.

Direct vs. Indirect Costs

Besides fixed and variable costs, we can also view expenses as direct and indirect. **Direct costs** include expenses we can directly attribute or trace to a specific patient, department, service, or cost center. Things like clinician salaries, procedure-related supplies, patient equipment, and patient transportation (in a hospital setting). These costs are *directly* tied to delivering specific services.

Indirect costs include expenses that cannot be directly tied to individual patients, services, or departments. Examples of these costs include general facility overhead like utilities, administrative salaries, shared services like medical records, and depreciation of buildings and equipment. Since indirect costs cannot be directly allocated, departments distribute them using allocation methods like square footage.

This may seem to be a distinction without a true difference. But key differences do exist.

- Companies can link direct costs to specific outputs. Indirect costs cannot.

- Direct costs are volume variable. Indirect costs are fixed or **step-variable**.

- Understanding direct costs per unit is key for service line margin analysis.

- Allocating indirect costs requires rules for spreading overhead.

So why does the distinction between direct and indirect costs matter? Understanding the difference between direct and indirect costs is crucial for effectively allocating overhead costs across departments, centers, and service lines (known as cost allocation). **Unit costing** analyzes the direct costs per unit of service (e.g., CPT code, patient day) and helps manage margins and optimize delivery costs. Budgets have more precision when built around direct costs per activity and then adding indirect cost allocations. Direct costs provide better metrics for evaluating organizational units and service lines by tying costs to outputs. Analyzing components of direct care costs and clinical variations often helps identify opportunities for cost reduction. Lastly, reimbursement from payers primarily aims to cover direct patient care costs.

Direct versus indirect costs for a rehabilitation department

Direct costs:

- Therapist salaries for patient care time

- Medical supplies used in treatment sessions

- Patient equipment like weights or pulleys

- Patient transportation services

Indirect costs:

- Department manager salary

- General liability insurance

- Facility maintenance and utilities

- Electronic medical record system

The rehabilitation center can attribute the direct costs to specific patients and services delivered. Indirect costs support general operations, but they cannot be linked to individual patients. The rehabilitation center can analyze the direct costs per therapy hour to understand and manage the expenses directly involved in care delivery. The department allocates indirect costs based on factors like square footage to cover shared overhead.

Productivity

Rehabilitation **productivity** is the efficient utilization of resources to achieve optimal patient outcomes, encompassing both individual provider efficiency and system-level resource allocation. We typically measure productivity by dividing the output (visits, services, revenue) by the input (time, effort, resources used). Further, there are two types of productivity, system- and individual-level. **System-level productivity** is the efficiency with which a hospital or outpatient rehab clinic treats patients. **Individual-level productivity** is how efficiently each therapist can treat those patients.

System-Level Productivity

At the organizational level—whether that is a hospital, department, or clinic—there are several types of common productivity indicators used.

Profit

We introduced **profit** in the first chapter of this text, but it requires a closer inspection in terms of productivity. While profitability is not a direct measure of productivity, it can offer indirect insights into the efficiency and effectiveness of a rehab program. We can define profit in a hospital, department, or rehab business as the excess of revenue over expenses. This definition of profit is the most common and essentially refers to the amount of money remaining after a business has covered all its costs. Profit is also the financial benefit realized when revenue generated from a business activity exceeds the expenses, costs, and taxes involved in sustaining the activity. This definition emphasizes the idea that profit is not just about generating income, but also about managing costs and considering different financial factors.

To sustain and grow, businesses require profit. It allows businesses to reinvest in themselves, innovate, and expand their operations. There are different types of profit, such as gross profit, operating profit, and net profit, each representing a different stage in the calculation of total profit. The pursuit of profit can sometimes lead to ethical concerns, such as prioritizing profit over social responsibility or environmental sustainability. Measuring and managing profit effectively is crucial for any business success and depends on the rehab setting.

Outpatient Rehab Profitability

Profitability for outpatient departments and clinics differs from inpatient or hospital profitability. Outpatient centers focus on several things, like return on assets (ROA), which was covered in Chapter 1. It may also include revenue per provider, which is the total revenue divided by the number of providers; this indicates revenue generation per clinician.

Example of Profitability in Outpatient Rehab

An outpatient rehab clinic has 10 physical therapists and 2 occupational therapists. The clinic generates $1,000,000 in total revenue for a specific month.

Calculation:

$Total\ Number\ of\ Providers = 10\ PT + 2\ OT$

$$= 12\ providers$$

$$Revenue\ per\ Provider = \frac{\$1,000,000}{12}$$

$$= \$83,333.33$$

Interpretation:

In this example, the average revenue per provider for the month is $83,333.33. This shows the average amount of revenue generated by each physical therapist and occupational therapist at the clinic. It's important to note that this is just an average and that the individual revenue for each provider may vary depending on factors like the number of patients seen; providers with higher patient volume often generate more revenue.

Increased Profitability can indicate:

- **Efficient resource utilization**—lower operating costs and minimal waste can contribute to higher profits, suggesting efficient use of staff, equipment, and other resources,

- **Effective service delivery**—higher patient volume and satisfaction, potentially due to efficient scheduling, quality care, and positive patient outcomes, leading to greater demand for services, or

- **Strategic pricing and negotiation**—higher profitability could reflect effective negotiation with insurance companies for favorable reimbursement rates or strategic pricing decisions that balance affordability with profitability.

There are limitations to using profitability as a productivity measure. The focus on financial outcome prioritizes the financial sustainability of the program, not necessarily patient outcomes or clinical excellence. In addition, factors beyond productivity, such as market competition, payer mix, and the overall healthcare environment, influence profitability, making it difficult to isolate the impact of pure efficiency as a productivity measure. Focusing solely on profitability might reward prioritizing lower cost treatments or minimizing services, potentially compromising the quality of care and patient outcomes. Therefore, we should use Outpatient Rehab Profitability cautiously as a measure of productivity. While it can provide indirect insights into efficiency and effectiveness, it's crucial to consider other factors like patient outcomes, clinical quality, and patient satisfaction for a more comprehensive understanding of the program's true productivity.

Hospital Department Profitability

Inpatient settings differ from outpatient settings in that they often look at productivity at more of an interdepartmental level. Most of their revenue is directly or indirectly tied to discharges. Examples for inpatient settings include:

- **Profit per discharge**—Departmental net income divided by total discharges. Profit generated per patient stay.

- **Net revenue per adjusted discharge**—Departmental net revenue divided by case mix adjusted discharges. Controls for patient complexity.

- **Profit per patient day**—revenue earned for each patient per day.

- **Labor cost as a percentage of revenue**—Labor expense divided by total revenue. Monitors staffing efficiency.

- **Direct margin per RVU**—(Revenue-direct costs) divided by total RVUs. Profitability per workload.

These are all useful examples that demonstrate metrics tailored to clinical settings for evaluating financial productivity.

Here are some examples with explanations of each hospital financial metric.

Profit per Discharge

A hospital department has a net income of $1,000,000 for a month.

During the same month, the department had 100 patient discharges.

$$Profit\ per\ Discharge = \frac{Departmental\ Net\ Income}{Total\ Discharges}$$

$$= \frac{\$1,000,000}{100\ discharges}$$

$$= \$10,000$$

This metric indicates the *average profit generated* for each patient discharged from a specific department within a specific timeframe.

Net Revenue per Adjusted Discharge (Case Mix Adjusted)

A hospital department has a net revenue of $1,200,000 for a month.

The department has 100 discharges, with a case mix adjustment factor of 1.1 (meaning the patients were slightly more complex than average).

$$Net\ Revenue\ per\ Adjusted\ Discharge = \frac{Departmental\ Net\ Revenue}{Case\ Mix\ Adjusted\ Discharges}$$

$$= \frac{\$1,200,000}{(100 \times 1.1)}$$

$$= \$10,909.09$$

This metric accounts for *patient complexity* by adjusting for the severity of illness and resource utilization. It provides a more accurate picture of revenue generated based on the actual care provided, compared to simply looking at unadjusted discharges.

Profit per Patient Day

A hospital department has a total revenue of $1,200,000 and 100 discharges for a month.

The average length of stay for patients in the department is 5 days.

$$Profit\ per\ Patient\ Day = \frac{Revenue\ per\ patient}{Average\ Length\ of\ Stay}$$

$$= \frac{(\$1{,}200{,}000 \div Total\ Discharges)}{Average\ Length\ of\ Stay}$$

$$= \frac{(\$1{,}200{,}000 \div 100)}{5.0\ days}$$

$$= \$2{,}400$$

This metric shows the *average profit generated per day* a patient stays in the department. It helps assess the efficiency of care delivery and resource utilization within the department.

Labor Cost as a Percentage of Revenue

A hospital has a total labor expense of $5,000,000 for a month.

The hospital generates a total revenue of $10,000,000 during the same month.

$$abor\ Cost\ as\ Percentage\ of\ Revenue = \frac{Labor\ Expense}{Total\ Revenue} \times 100$$

$$= \frac{\$5{,}000{,}000}{\$10{,}000{,}000} \times 100$$

$$= 50\%$$

This metric shows the *percentage of total revenue spent on labor costs.* It helps assess staffing efficiency and identify areas for potential cost savings.

Direct Margin per RVU (Relative Value Unit)

A hospital department generates $1,000,000 in revenue for a month.

The department incurs $200,000 in direct costs (costs directly associated with patient care) during the same month.

The department performs 1,000 RVUs worth of work (a unit reflecting the complexity and resources used in providing specific services).

$$Margin\ per\ RVU = \frac{(Revnue - Direct\ Costs)}{Total\ RVUs}$$

$$= \frac{(\$1{,}000{,}000 - \$200{,}000)}{1{,}000\ RVUs}$$

$$= \$800$$

This metric shows the *profit generated per unit of work performed* (measured in RVUs) after accounting for direct costs. It helps assess the profitability of specific services and identifies areas for improvement in service delivery or reimbursement rates.

Note: It is important to analyze these metrics in context and consider them alongside other relevant factors for a comprehensive understanding of a hospital's financial performance.

Margin

The most frequently used measure of profitability for both inpatient and outpatient settings is margin. Margin is like profit, but there are differences. Whereas profit is an absolute dollar amount, margin is usually a percentage. Profit is what a company earns, while margin provides a relative measure of efficiency or profitability. Each rehab entity is unique, however; some may combine these two and use the terms interchangeably. As in some specific contexts, *margin* can refer to a specific dollar amount representing the difference between two values. This is less common, but specific industries or situations may use margin in this way.

We can use several types of margins to analyze profits. The three margins introduced in chapter one include gross profit margin, operating profit margin, and net profit margin. Two other margins are contribution margin and profit or product margin.

Contribution Margin (CM)

Contribution margin is the value that is left to contribute towards any fixed cost and then the desired profit. CM is not profit, however. Instead, it is the amount left over after covering all *variable* (incremental) costs. We still need to cover the fixed costs. It is easiest to think of the contribution margin equation as:

$$total\ contribution\ margin = total\ revenue - total\ variable\ cost$$

OR

$$contribution\ margin\ per\ unit\ = revenue\ per\ unit - variable\ cost\ per\ unit$$

If the CM per unit is positive, then rehab leaders should continue to provide the service. If the CM per unit is negative, however, it is not in the organization's best financial interest to continue to provide the service.

Ceteris paribus is a Latin phrase that generally means "all other things being equal." Here, it acts as a shorthand indication of the effect one economic variable has on another, provided all other variables remain the same.

This is a crucial concept in economics and business used to isolate the impact of a specific variable on an outcome while assuming all other factors remain unchanged. In discussing contribution and profit margins, *ceteris paribus* helps us understand the impact of changes in specific variables on these margins while assuming other factors impacting them stay constant. Here are some examples:

Analyzing the impact of pricing changes on contribution margin.

By holding fixed costs, variable costs per unit, and sales volume constant, we can use *ceteris paribus* to isolate the effect of increasing or decreasing the selling price on the contribution margin. This allows us to assess the profitability of potential pricing strategies without the influence of other variables.

Evaluating the effect of cost reductions on profit margin.

By assuming fixed costs, selling price, and sales volume remain constant, we can use *ceteris paribus* to understand the impact of reducing variable costs per unit on the profit margin. This helps identify areas for cost optimization and potential improvements in overall profitability.

Examining the relationship between volume discounts and contribution margin.

Holding fixed costs, variable cost per unit, and original selling price constant, we can use *ceteris paribus* to analyze the contribution margin implications of offering volume discounts. This allows us to assess the trade-off between increased sales volume and potential reduction in contribution margin per unit.

Note: *Ceteris paribus* is a theoretical construct and doesn't reflect real-world scenarios where multiple factors often change simultaneously. However, it serves as a valuable tool for isolating the effect of specific variables on financial metrics like contribution and profit margins, allowing for better decision making and strategic planning in business operations.

Product (Profit) Margin

The **product (or profit) margin**[1] is the value remaining after all variable and avoidable fixed costs have been incurred only because a service is being provided. **Avoidable fixed costs** are the fixed or overhead costs that could be eliminated or avoided if a particular service line or business unit was discontinued. Rent and salaries are examples of avoidable fixed costs. The key factor is that these fixed overhead costs are attributable to the specific business segment in question and could be *avoided* if that segment no longer existed. By incorporating avoidable fixed costs into product margin analysis, managers gain a more comprehensive view of the net profitability of that product or service line when making strategic business decisions. This provides advantages over only looking at the contribution margin.

Like contribution margin, there are equations for product margin as well.

product margin = total contribution margin − avoidable fixed costs

If the PM is positive, then rehab leaders should continue to provide the service. If the PM is negative, however, it is not in the organization's best financial interest to continue to provide the service.

Contribution Margin vs. Product Margin

The contribution margin differs from the gross profit margin, the difference between sales revenue and the cost of goods sold. While contribution margins only count the variable costs, the gross profit margin includes all the costs that a company incurs in order to make sales.

---

1. Note: In this book, we will use the terms "product margin" and "profit margin" interchangeably, referring to both concepts as "product margin." While there are technical differences between the two metrics, as discussed in the previous sections, it is not uncommon for professionals to use these terms synonymously in certain contexts.

The contribution margin shows how much additional revenue the company generates by producing each additional unit of product after reaching the breakeven point. In other words, it measures how much money each additional sale "contributes" to the company's total profits.

The profit margin is the amount of revenue left after deducting the direct production costs. Contribution margin is a measure of the profitability of each individual product that a business sells.

Here are examples demonstrating contribution margin and product margin calculations for a rehabilitation service line:

Revenue for outpatient clinic: $1,500,000

Variable costs:

Medical supplies: $200,000

Billing fees: $50,000

Total variable costs: $250,000

Fixed costs:

Clinician salaries: $600,000

Rent: $150,000

Total fixed costs: $750,000

$Contribution\ Margin = Revenue - Variable\ Costs$

$= \$1,500,000 - \$250,000$

$= \$1,250,000$

Avoidable fixed costs:

Clinic medical director salary: $120,000

Dedicated billing staff: $50,000

Total avoidable fixed costs: $170,000

$Product\ Margin = Contribution\ Margin - Avoidable\ Fixed\ Costs$

$= \$1,250,000 - \$170,000$

$= \$1,080,000$

A rehabilitation clinic or department has two primary ways to increase contribution margins, increase revenues or decrease variable costs.

The clinic can generate more revenue per patient by:

- Renegotiating higher reimbursement rates from insurance payers.

- Maximizing billing capture of allowable charges.

- Improving documentation and coding to support higher acuity billing.

- Offering self-pay services not covered by insurance.

- Using co-treatments and group therapies to increase revenue per visit.

- Gaining higher patient volumes through referrals, marketing, and new services.

However, taking on too many patients could decrease quality or require more staffing expenses. So, we need to find a balance.

The clinic can reduce variable costs per patient visit by:

- Negotiating discounts on frequently used medical supplies and equipment,

- Adjusting staffing ratios and therapist mixes to optimize labor efficiency,

- Leveraging support personnel for documentation and non-clinical tasks,

- Monitoring and reducing waste of clinical consumable materials, or

- Standardizing procedures to eliminate unnecessary variability in supplies.

The key is boosting revenue per visit and reducing variable costs per visit to realize the maximum contribution margin. This provides more dollars to cover fixed overhead and generate bottom line profits.

Volume

Length of Stay

Length of stay (LOS) measures the duration of a patient's hospital admission from the time of admission to discharge and is a key metric of hospital productivity, utilization, and patient flow. Shorter LOS allows hospitals to treat more patients with available beds, improving volume productivity. Further, while some patients may require longer stays for complex cases, unnecessary prolongations can be frustrating and contribute to lower patient satisfaction.

Long LOS times directly translate to higher overall treatment costs for the facility and can increase costs as patients occupy beds and resources unnecessarily. This can affect both the hospital's budget and patient bills while also tying up capacity and limiting new admissions. In addition, the longer a patient stays in the hospital, the higher the risk of contracting healthcare-acquired infections (HAIs), leading to additional complications and costs.

Measuring Length of Stay

We commonly measure length of stay in one of two ways, the average length of stay (ALOS) and geometric mean length of stay (GMLOS). ALOS measures the average duration across all patient admissions and discharges during a period and GMLOS calculates the average LOS accounting for the statistical distribution of stays. GMLOS prevents extremely short or long outliers from skewing the average.

Some differences between the two:

- ALOS is easier to calculate but more sensitive to extremes. GMLOS is more statistically stable.

- GMLOS will typically be lower than ALOS for a given patient population.

- ALOS can overstate the central tendency if long stay outliers are present.

- GMLOS better represents the "typical" expected stay.

- GMLOS is recommended for comparing LOS over time or across units.

Length of Stay Formulae

ALOS

$$ALOS = \frac{Total\ Inpatient\ Days}{Total\ Admissions}$$

GMLOS

$$GMLOS = n\sqrt{(LOS1 \times LOS2 \times \ldots LOSn)}$$

OR

$$GMLOS = exp(\frac{(\Sigma\ ln(LOSi))}{n})$$

Where:

Σ: Summation symbol (represents adding up the values for all patients)

$ln(LOSi)$: Natural logarithm of the length of stay for each patient (i)

n: Total number of patients

For example:

Let's say we have data for 5 hospital admissions with the following lengths of stay:

Patient	Length o' Stay
Patient 1	3
Patient 2	5
Patient 3	2
Patient 4	8
Patient 5	1

ALOS:

$$ALOS = \frac{Total\ Inpatient\ Days}{Total\ Admissions}$$

$$= \frac{3+5+2+8+1}{5}$$

$$= 3.8\ days$$

GMLOS:

$$GMLOS = (3 \times 5 \times 2 \times 8 \times 1)^{\frac{1}{5}}$$

$$= 3.1\ days$$

The ALOS (3.8 days) provides a simple average of individual lengths of stay, potentially skewed by outliers like patient 4 (8 days). The GMLOS (3.1 days) reduces the influence of outliers by taking the geometric mean, offering a more robust measure of central tendency in this case. This highlights the potential limitations of solely relying on ALOS. GMLOS offers a better representation of the typical length of stay for this specific sample by reducing the impact of extreme values.

Length of stay is similar to patient days, but it is a different measure. **Patient days** tracks the total number of days patients spend in all hospital beds during a time period. It is calculated by summing all inpatient days for each admission during the timeframe. It provides a measure of overall hospital volume and bed utilization but doesn't account for length of each stay or provide average duration. LOS measures the duration from admission to discharge for each patient stay and provides information on efficiency of care and patient throughput.

Feature	Description	Example
Average Length of Stay (LOS)	Average number of days a patient stays in the hospital per admission.	Three patients stay in the hospital for 3, 4, and 5 days. The ALOS is 4.0 ($12\ days \div 3\ patients = 4.0\ ALOS$)
Patient Days	Total number of days all patients spend in the hospital during a specific period.	In a week, a hospital has 10 patients with an average LOS of 3 days. The total patient days would be 30 ($10\ patients \times 3\ days = 30\ patient\ days$)

Patient days measures *total* volume while LOS evaluates the duration of *individual* hospitalizations. Assessing both metrics provides insights into hospital utilization, productivity, and patient flow.

We can improve LOS by enhancing patient mobility, refining clinical protocols, coordinating care, planning discharges, and transitioning patients to home health or rehab facilities when appropriate.

CMS Incentives to Reduce LOS

The rise of diagnosis-related groups (DRGs) introduced case-rate payments to encourage hospitals to contain costs and optimize LOS for each admission. The Hospital Readmissions Reduction Program penalizes hospitals with high readmission rates for certain conditions; the goal with this is to drive improvement. Bundled payments for episodes of care also reward providers for working together to achieve more efficient care and shorter LOS when appropriate.

Length of stay is a critical hospital productivity metric. Monitoring ALOS and GMLOS helps identify opportunities to improve bed throughput, lower costs, and incentivize efficient, quality care.

Intensity

Intensity of patients is best measured in a hospital with the case mix index (CMI); CMI measures the clinical complexity and resource intensity of patients treated at a healthcare facility. It is used to quantify how "sick" the patient population is based on diagnostic and treatment factors. To calculate CMI, we add the relative weight of each patient's diagnosis-related group (DRG) and divide it by the number of cases. The relative weight reflects expected resource utilization for that DRG. Higher weights indicate greater complexity. A CMI of 1.0 reflects average complexity. Higher CMI indicates sicker, more resource *intense* patients. CMI adjusts for severity differences when comparing utilization, costs, and outcomes across facilities. We would expect a hospital with a higher CMI to have higher costs per discharge and potentially higher mortality rates due to treating more complex cases. Because of this, CMS incorporates CMI adjustments into their Hospital Value-Based Purchasing program when evaluating facility performance.

Efficiency

Efficiency in a hospital refers to the ability to use resources productively in delivering patient care, maximizing the quantity and quality of services provided given the available costs and constraints. There are many ways to measure efficiency, here are some metrics related to staffing, labor, and service utilization:

- **Inpatient FTEs per Unit Bed**—This calculates the number of full-time equivalent inpatient staff per each staffed bed. A lower ratio indicates more efficient staffing aligned to bed utilization.

- **Hours per Patient Day**—This measures the total staff hours worked divided by the total patient days. A lower number means staff hours are being used more efficiently per each day of patient care.

- **Units of Service per Labor Hour**—This measurement quantifies the number of billable tests, procedures, or other services that the staff provides per hour of work. A higher number reflects greater workforce productivity in delivering patient services.

- **Discharges per Bed**—Higher discharges per bed indicates beds are being turned over more quickly through efficient treatment and discharge planning.

- **Revenue per FTE**—This measures total revenue generated per each full-time staff. Improving revenue per FTE means staff are contributing more to the hospital's financial performance.

- **Overtime Costs**—Monitoring overtime costs as a percentage of total salary spending helps identify workflow inefficiencies requiring excessive overtime.

Tracking metrics like these over time and benchmarking against other hospitals helps manage the efficient utilization of resources—staff, beds, and finances—in delivering high-quality care.

Unit cost

Unit cost refers to the average expenditure required to produce each quantifiable unit of care or service, such as the cost per day, admission, procedure, test, or clinic visit. Tracking unit costs helps healthcare organizations assess resource utilization efficiency and productivity in delivering services.

Here are some examples of how hospitals can measure unit costs:

- **Salary per FTE**—This calculates the average employee salary expense by taking total salaries divided by the number of full—time equivalent staff. It helps monitor labor costs.

- **Cost per Patient Day**—This measures the average cost to provide care per patient day. To calculate it, we take the total expenses and divide it by the total patient days provided. This helps track resource utilization.

- **Cost per Discharge**—Similar to cost per patient day but specifically for inpatient discharges. Calculated by taking total inpatient costs divided by number of discharges. Measures inpatient care efficiency.

- **Cost per Procedure**—Looks at the total direct costs of a treatment or test divided by the number of procedures performed. Helps manage procedural resource utilization.

- **Cost per Clinic Visit**—Calculates the total costs of running a clinic divided by the number of visits provided. Assesses outpatient care costs.

Monitoring these unit costs over time and comparing them to benchmarks helps hospitals manage resource allocation and optimize delivery of care. The goal is maximizing the volume and quality of services provided within the available budget constraints. Lowering the cost per unit of service improves overall efficiency.

Individual-Level Productivity

While crucial for assessing system-level efficiency, traditional profitability metrics may have limitations. Tracking individual therapist productivity offers a deeper dive, allowing health systems and clinics to refine resource allocation, identify areas for improvement, and ultimately optimize patient care, complementing system-level insights for a more comprehensive understanding of productivity. Productivity metrics for therapists consider patient caseload, billable units per visit, and discharge status. Ensuring optimal productivity and minimizing unnecessary costs is crucial with constrained reimbursement rates. For individual clinicians, key productivity metrics are volume, units, revenue, utilization, and efficiency.

Volume

Volume is the number of patients a therapist sees per day or per week in the clinic. Monitoring therapist volume is important for ensuring patient access and maximizing revenue capacity. Higher volumes reflect the demand for services.

However, volume alone can be misleading when evaluating productivity. Therapists may see high volumes of patients but bill few units of service per patient because of inefficient documentation or misuse of codes. Volume also doesn't account for complexity, i.e., more complex patients require more time and therefore volumes are lower. High volumes could indicate rushed care rather than efficiency.

The optimal balance considers volume alongside metrics like units billed per patient encounter and minutes per unit to ensure both capacity and documentation quality. Excessive volume is counterproductive if it detracts from revenue capture or patient outcomes.

Volume is an important but incomplete productivity measure for therapists. To prevent misleading conclusions or unintended consequences to quality of care, one should analyze it in tandem with other metrics.

Units

Therapists deliver interventions that are billed based on CPT (Current Procedural Terminology) codes; these codes are used to bill for rehabilitation services. Each code represents a type of intervention or evaluation. Many CPT codes for therapies are *timed based* on 15-minute increments of direct treatment. For example, code 97110 for therapeutic exercise is billed in 15-minute increments or **units**. 30 minutes is equivalent to 2 units, 45 minutes is equivalent to 3 units, and so on. Other examples of timed codes are 97112 (neuromuscular reeducation) and 97530 (therapeutic activities). Non-timed CPT codes are billed as one unit, regardless of the time spent. Examples of these include evaluation s—e.g., 97161 is the CPT code for a low complexity physical therapy evaluation—and some modalities—e.g., 97014 is the CPT code for unattended electrical stimulation. Therapists should bill untimed codes as one unit, regardless of time spent.

Tracking the number of units of CPT codes—both timed and untimed—billed per visit for each therapist is a key productivity measure.

It is possible to compare units billed by individual therapists with national averages. Benchmarking typical units billed may help identify therapists missing revenue opportunities through under-coding services delivered. For example, the average units billed per visit typically ranges from 3 to 5 units. One challenge of comparing individual therapists to normative values is the possibility of over billing for services. Therapists must align units billed to established coding guidelines and support them with treatment documentation. Unethical coding to inflate units jeopardizes compliance.

Including the number of units billed adds to the productivity picture for therapists, as volume alone does not determine productivity. A high-volume therapist billing fewer units per visit may actually be less productive. Along with volume, monitoring units billed per visit provides a more complete picture of individual therapist productivity in outpatient rehabilitation settings. It can highlight documentation and billing improvement opportunities.

Revenue

We can also track revenue and use this to measure productivity for outpatient rehabilitation therapists. Net patient service revenue—NPSR—attributable to each therapist should be tracked. Gross revenue—GPSR—can also be tracked and often is; however, we need to remember that GPSR does not represent the monies collected from each visit.

We calculate revenue per encounter by dividing NPSR by the number of visits. Higher revenue per visit reflects more accurate coding and better billing capture. We track revenue per episode of care to assess our ability to maximize reimbursement for a patient's entire course of care. Optimizing revenue as a measure of productivity helps offset restrictions in reimbursement rates and payer mix. But quality of care and documentation integrity must remain priorities; *upcoding* to increase revenue is unethical and illegal.

Hours Worked

To provide the most complete picture, we need to combine each of these measurements (i.e., visits, units, revenue) with the number of hours worked. **Hours worked** is simply the time each therapist is being paid; others may refer to this as billable hours, scheduled hours, or labor hours, but for our purposes, it will be *hours worked*. Therapists who work fewer hours but see more patients and bill more units are more productive than therapists who work more hours but see fewer patients and bill fewer units. Below are some examples of how to analyze patient visits, units billed, revenue, and hours worked together to evaluate productivity for outpatient rehabilitation therapists.

Visits per hour worked

Calculates the number of patient encounters per hour worked. Assesses efficiency in delivering care.

Example:

25 visits per week

20 hours worked

$$Visits\ per\ hour = \frac{visits}{hours\ worked}$$
$$= \frac{25\ visits}{20\ hours\ worked}$$
$$= 1.25\ visits\ per\ hour\ worked$$

Units per hour worked

Measures the number of billable units per hour. Higher indicates better billing documentation and capture.

Example:

35 units billed per week

20 hours worked

$$Units\ per\ hour = \frac{units}{hours\ worked}$$

$$= \frac{35\ units}{20\ hours\ worked}$$

$$= 1.75\ units\ per\ hour$$

Revenue per hour worked

Total revenue generated per hour worked. Accounts for both utilization and billing effectiveness.

Example:

$2,000 revenue (NPSR) per week

20 hours worked

$$Revenue\ per\ hour\ worked = \frac{NPSR}{hours\ worked}$$

$$= \frac{\$2,000}{20\ hours\ worked}$$

$$= \$100\ per\ hour\ worked$$

Hours worked per unit of service

The inverse of units per hour. Lower hours per unit demonstrates greater time efficiency.

Example:

35 units per week

20 hours worked

$$Hours\ worked\ per\ unit\ of\ service = \frac{hours\ worked}{units\ billed}$$

$$= \frac{20\ hours\ worked}{35\ units\ of\ service}$$

$$= 0.57\ hours\ worked\ per\ unit\ of\ service$$

Analyzing metrics together in this way provides a more complete picture of productivity and helps identify potential areas for improvement. The goal is optimizing utilization, revenue, compliance, and efficiency simultaneously.

Productivity Dashboard. A visual representation of the monthly key productivity metrics for a rehabilitation department.

Embracing Anti-Productivity for Optimal Outcomes

Having explored both system—level and individual—level productivity measures, it's valuable to consider the concept of "anti-productivity." Setting productivity standards and monitoring clinician performance against benchmarks helps maximize capacity and revenue; we must also ensure our workforce works in an environment that emphasizes physical and mental safety. This allows our therapists with a greater ability to provide quality care. **Anti-productivity** challenges the focus on constant output, recognizing that seemingly unproductive activities like therapist self-care or preventative care can ultimately enhance long-term efficiency and patient outcomes. While it may seem contradictory, this idea questions the conventional approach of prioritizing maximum output without considering the drawbacks.

Examples of anti-productivity in healthcare might include:

- Therapist self-care. While scheduling time for mental and physical wellbeing might appear unproductive, a well-rested and energized therapist can deliver better care, potentially leading to fewer patient cancellations and improved outcomes.

- Investing in preventative care. Spending time on preventative measures like patient education or early intervention strategies could appear less productive compared to treating acute conditions. However, it can ultimately reduce overall healthcare costs and improve population health.

- Strategic use of technology. Implementing new technologies can involve an initial learning curve and disruption to workflows. However, the long-term benefits of automation, data analysis, or improved communication can significantly improve overall efficiency.

Addressing anti-productivity requires a *shift in perspective*. Healthcare systems and clinics should embrace a holistic view of productivity by recognizing the value of activities that enhance long-term sustainability and quality, even if they don't translate directly into immediate output gains. Investments in staff well-being fosters a culture that encourages breaks, professional development, and work-life balance, understanding that a happy and healthy workforce is a productive one.

Focusing on outcomes, not just outputs, allows us to evaluate success not just by the number of patients seen but also by patient satisfaction, long-term health outcomes, and cost-effectiveness. With *Value-Based Care*, balancing productivity and quality is critical. The focus expands from volume alone to value per patient, so analytics should tie clinician productivity to outcomes. This is where outcomes and quality of care matter. It is beyond the scope of this text to review outcomes, but ultimately, patient health outcomes reflect the end results of the therapy provided and outcomes indicate the quality and efficacy of services.

Common outcomes tracked include things like improvement in pain, range of motion, strength, balance, mobility, speech & language skills, and the ability to perform activities of daily living. While not a direct productivity metric, better outcomes suggest the therapist is providing skilled, efficient, and effective interventions tailored to the patient's needs. Therapists focused solely on volume or revenue metrics could inadvertently skimp on care quality and individual customization required to achieve strong outcomes. Monitoring outcomes ensures therapists balance productivity goals with service quality and patient benefit. However, outcomes are impacted by many factors beyond the therapist's control like patient adherence and health status. So patient-reported outcomes cannot be the sole productivity measure.

By acknowledging and integrating "anti-productive" activities into a broader framework, healthcare systems and clinics can optimize productivity for the ultimate goal, which is to deliver high-quality, sustainable patient care.

Conclusion

Productivity is vital for healthcare organizations to maximize value and optimize scarce resources. At the system level, key metrics include profitability, costs, utilization, patient throughput, and care quality. Monitoring unit costs, analyzing fixed versus variable expenses, and leveraging benchmarks helps manage efficiency. For individual clinicians, important productivity measures relate to volume, revenue, procedure units billed, and patient outcomes balanced against integrity and quality. As reimbursement models shift toward value-based care, the focus must expand from productivity alone to also consider the benefit for patients per unit of resource spent. A data-driven approach to measuring productivity at both organization and clinician levels provides crucial insights to improve fiscal performance, utilization, and quality within healthcare's shifting payment landscape.

As Amanda and Ella wrap up their productivity brainstorming session, she can't help but feel energized. "Who knew that efficiency could be so exhilarating?" She grins, already planning the first annual "Productivity Olympics" in her head.

Personal Reflection: Amanda realizes that productivity is not just about working harder; it's about working smarter and creating a culture of continuous improvement. She learns the importance of involving her team in the process, setting clear goals, and celebrating successes along the way. She commits to leading by example and to empowering her staff to find innovative ways to maximize their time and talents.

Chapter Five

Revenue Generation in Rehabilitation

Amanda's got revenue generation on the brain, and she's ready to think outside the box—or the therapy gym, in this case. She's pretty sure that "diversifying revenue streams" doesn't mean installing a chocolate fountain in the lobby, but she's open to creative ideas. In a meeting with her leadership team, Amanda channels her inner entrepreneur.

"Alright, team, it's time to get creative! We need to find new ways to bring in revenue, and I'm not talking about selling lemonade in the parking lot," Amanda grins, as her team chuckles.

The outpatient supervisor, Sunni, pipes up,
"What about offering a 'Yoga for Couch Potatoes' class? We could market it as a gentle introduction to physical activity for those who
think 'namaste' is a fancy way to say 'no, thank
you' to exercise."

The occupational therapy supervisor, John,
chimes in, "Or we could partner with local
businesses to offer 'Ergonomics 101' work-
shops, teaching people how to set up their
workstations to avoid the dreaded 'keyboard
hunch.'"

As the ideas flow, Amanda feels a surge of excitement. With a little creativity and a lot of
hustle, she knows they can generate additional
revenue streams while still staying true to their
mission of helping patients live their best lives.

The sustainability and profitability of rehab clinics and hospital—based departments depend heavily on their ability to generate revenue. Regardless of the setting, the saying, "no money, no mission" applies. This chapter outlines approaches to
optimizing revenue streams through service line development, pricing strategies, payer
mix management, and new revenue opportunities.

Service Line Development

Traditional rehab clinics offer standard orthopedic care, treatment of chronic conditions,
and post-surgical rehabilitation. These are all important patient types to treat, and most

patients respond quite well to the interventions provided by these physical and occupational therapists. When several clinics in an area offer the same programming, however, **provider saturation** presents a challenge for those trying to stand apart from other area clinics. While there are several strategies to be noticeable, developing a niche service—or multiple niches—is one way to differentiate one practice from another. Expanding service offerings that address unmet needs in the community can drive additional revenue. Several nontraditional service lines exist that may help clinics and departments increase revenue.

Provider saturation refers to the *density of healthcare providers* offering a specific service within a defined geographic area *relative to the number of patients* who might benefit from those services.

Here's a breakdown of the key aspects:

- **Density of Providers**. This refers to the number of providers (e.g., doctors, therapists) available in a specific area.

- **Geographic Area**. This could be a city, county, state, or even a specific hospital department.

- **Service**. This refers to the *particular type of healthcare service* being provided (e.g., cardiology, physical therapy).

- **Beneficiary Population**. This represents the *number of patients* who might require or benefit from the specific healthcare service.

Essentially, provider saturation indicates whether there are:

1. Too few providers to serve the population's needs adequately, potentially resulting in long wait times and limited access to care,

2. Enough providers to meet the population's demand for the service, or

3. Too many providers in the area, potentially leading to competition for patients and potentially affecting the financial sustainability of practices.

Understanding provider saturation is crucial for healthcare policymakers, administrators, and even individual providers to make informed decisions about:

- **Resource allocation**. Distributing healthcare resources like equipment and personnel to address areas with provider shortages.

- **Practice location**. Providers considering setting up practice in a new area can use provider saturation data to assess potential patient demand and competition.

- **Service expansion**. Existing healthcare facilities can use this data to determine if there's enough demand to expand the range of services offered.

Some data sources for analyzing provider saturation may include government agencies for population and demographic data, healthcare insurance companies for payer mix, and professional organizations for the number of area providers.

By analyzing provider saturation, healthcare stakeholders can work towards ensuring *optimal access to quality care* for the population.

What follows are several service lines that may help rehab clinics and hospital departments provide services that the community may desire. This serves as an introduction to these services; it is recommended that you review other sources of information prior to starting such programs.

Vestibular Rehabilitation

This specialty focuses on the assessment and treatment of balance disorders, dizziness, and vertigo through targeted exercises, balance retraining, gaze stabilization, and desensitization techniques. It promotes central nervous system compensation for inner ear deficits that can cause significant instability and fall risk. There is a large unmet need for vestibular rehabilitation among aging populations susceptible to such vestibular and balance conditions. Vestibular therapy requires specialized training but offers a way to attract new patient populations through relationships with ENT physicians, neurologists, and audiologists.

Aquatic Therapy

Aquatic therapy provides physical therapy and therapeutic exercises performed in a pool rather than a clinic. The water buoyancy helps reduce weight-bearing and compression forces, enabling earlier mobility with less pain for acute injuries, arthritis, neurological conditions, or post-surgical recovery. While requiring investment in a therapeutic pool, aquatic therapy can attract new patients unwilling or unable to tolerate land-based physical therapy. It offers a potential revenue stream through memberships or classes in addition to 1-on-1 aquatic PT.

Hand Therapy

Hand therapy specializes in the rehabilitation of wrist, hand, and upper extremity injuries and conditions through modalities, manual techniques, custom splinting/orthotics, and specialized therapeutic exercises. Common diagnoses include sports injuries, arthritis, tendonitis, fractures, carpal tunnel syndrome, and nerve injuries. Advanced expertise in custom braces, splints, and other orthotic interventions provides a unique revenue stream beyond therapy alone. Partnerships—formal and informal—with orthopedic surgeons and hand specialists are key for referrals.

Cognitive Rehabilitation

Cognitive rehab helps rebuild mental skills and function for patients who suffered neurological impairment from brain injury, stroke, or other conditions. Services involve memory, attention, language, visual-spatial, and executive function therapies. Given the complexity of brain injuries, customized treatment plans are required. Demand is increasing with more awareness of concussions and other brain trauma. Collaborations with neurologists, neuropsychologists, schools, and brain injury programs offer referrals.

Oncology Rehabilitation

Oncology rehabilitation focuses on restoring strength, mobility, function, and quality of life to cancer patients during or after treatment. Goals involve overcoming fatigue, generalized weakness, neuropathy, pain, balance problems, and other deficits that can result from surgical interventions, chemotherapy, radiation, or advanced cancer. Rehabilitation helps counteract the often significant deconditioning and toxic effects of cancer therapies. Programming collaboration with oncologists, cancer centers, and patient advocacy groups provides a steady referral base as cancer prevalence rises and care improves. Specific training in the precautions, comorbidities, and needs of cancer patients is necessary, as well as emotional sensitivity. But this service line leverages the restoring care skills already present in outpatient therapy clinics.

Though often used interchangeably, oncology rehab is not exactly the same as survivorship, although they are closely related. Here's how to differentiate them.

Oncology Rehab

Focus: Focuses on *physical rehabilitation* following cancer treatment.

Goal: Aims to help patients *regain strength, function, and mobility* after surgery, radiation, or chemotherapy.

Target Audience: Primarily targets *cancer patients* who are actively undergoing or recovering from treatment.

Survivorship

Scope: A broader term encompassing *all aspects of a cancer patient's life* after diagnosis and treatment.

Focus: Includes physical rehabilitation (oncology rehab) but also extends to *psychosocial support, emotional wellbeing, managing long-term side effects, and navigating life after cancer.*

Target Audience: All *cancer survivors*, including those who may not require specific rehabilitation services but need support in other areas.

Oncology rehab is a crucial component of cancer survivorship programs. While oncology rehab focuses on physical recovery, survivorship encompasses the entire journey of a cancer survivor. Many cancer survivors benefit from both oncology rehab services and other survivorship programs. In summary, oncology rehab is a specific type of rehabilitation focused on physical recovery after cancer treatment, while survivorship is a broader concept that includes oncology rehab along with other support services for all cancer survivors throughout their journey.

Pediatric Rehabilitation

Developing a dedicated pediatric rehabilitation program offers significant potential, though requiring specialized training and facilities. Customizing services to the needs of infants, children, and adolescents with developmental delays, injuries, neurological conditions, or other special needs is a must. Staff must use family-centered, play-based approaches tuned appropriately to age and abilities. Partnerships with children's hospitals, NICUs, pediatric specialists, and community pediatricians are crucial for referrals. Revenue possibilities exist by participating in early intervention state programs. Schools also represent opportunities to provide therapy services. Specific expertise areas to cultivate include feeding issues, cerebral palsy, autism spectrum disorder, and neonatal intensive care unit graduate follow-up. While pediatric rehabilitation requires extra customization, the capabilities align well with the skills of existing therapists.

Pediatric rehabilitation takes two main approaches, *traditional* and *sport-related*. Traditional pediatric rehab focuses on congenital conditions or those arising during development, like cerebral palsy or muscular dystrophy. Here, therapists work on improving a child's overall motor skills, strength, and independence for daily life activities. In contrast, sport-related pediatric rehab addresses injuries sustained during youth sports participation. Therapists in this field help young athletes recover from sprains, strains, or overuse injuries, aiming for a safe and speedy return to their chosen sport.

Pelvic Health

Pelvic health services provide care for urinary/fecal incontinence, pelvic pain conditions, and other pelvic floor disorders through techniques like biofeedback, electrical stimulation, manual therapy, therapeutic exercises, and more. Given the sensitive nature, individualized treatment plans and client comfort are imperative. Specialized pelvic health training is required, but large patient demand exists.

Healthcare providers commonly offer therapies for pelvic floor dysfunction to women during or following pregnancy. This narrow view, however, ignores other females who might benefit from these services. Incontinence in children at night—i.e., bedwetting—is a unique offering. Many young—and older—female athletes are also incontinent when performing their sporting activities. Women and girls often view this form of stress incontinence as *normal*, but it is not. Instead, addressing it offers an opportunity to help an underserved population.

While typically viewed as a service only for women, males have pelvic issues as well; because this is less commonly focused upon, pelvic health therapies for men are a unique opportunity for a clinic or department looking to expand the diversity of its services. Marketing to OB/GYNs, urologists, primary care, and pediatric providers is crucial for referrals.

Sports Rehab

Developing sports therapy programs offers tremendous potential to attract new patients and revenue streams. Services can include sports performance training, injury recovery, concussion rehabilitation, and injury prevention services for athletes. Providing post-surgical rehabilitation for common procedures like ACL reconstruction is also valuable. Sports therapy can tap into demand from area schools, sports clubs, gyms, sports teams, individual athletes, and active adults. Offering cash-based custom exercise, gait and movement analysis, injury screening, and conditioning programs creates additional revenue beyond traditional therapy. Partnering with orthopedic surgeons, athletic trainers, coaches, and fitness facilities provides referral pipelines. Specialty certifications in sports rehabilitation lend credibility and expertise in marketing services. The possibilities in sports therapy are far-reaching in re-engaging patients for lifelong wellness beyond just recovery.

Expanded Wheelchair Seating & Custom Orthotics

Offering advanced wheelchair and seating evaluations plus custom orthotic fabrication provides a complementary service line fitting the rehab team's skills. Certified specialists assess wheelchair positioning, mobility, and pressure relief needs. Custom seating systems and mobility devices have a significant impact on patients' function, health, and quality of life. And fabricating custom orthotics, braces, and splints offers unique in-house revenue versus contracting out.

Thorough market analysis of competitors, referral demand, and payer coverage for new services is crucial before investing (see previous discussion of provider saturation). Further, service lines should align strategically with organizational goals.

Pricing Strategies

Tactical pricing approaches help maximize reimbursement rates allowed within constraints of payer contracts. One way to accomplish this is by establishing higher rates for self-pay patients to offset lower contracted rates from insurers. This can be done with traditional therapy services. But it may also be done with alternative revenue streams (discussed later in this chapter). Pricing ancillary self-pay services appropriately allows clinics to earn additional revenue from existing patients. Examples are massage, personal training, classes.

It is important to review payer contracts and renegotiate increases annually. Careful management of contract concessions may yield increased payments. Similarly, providers should adjust fee schedules annually by service type to optimize within reimbursement caps.

In addition, rehab clinic and department managers should ensure billing practices capture maximum allowable reimbursement. The Revenue Cycle Management chapter later in this book covers this topic.

Payer Mix Optimization

Managing the distribution of payers and aligning service offerings to match is imperative. Medicare and Medicaid traditionally reimburse at a lower rate than both self-pay and commercial payers. If a clinic's patient population was covered primarily by Medicare or Medicaid, revenues would be less than ideal. Service growth, then, should focus on areas with the highest reimbursement potential. Likewise, referral sources might restrict reimbursement by referring primarily Medicare- or Medicaid- insured patients; expanding volumes from providers who refer patients from commercial payers would be helpful to maximize revenues and reimbursement. However, this author believes we should not refuse care to patients with insurances that do not pay as well, such as Medicaid.

With value-based models emerging, the focus must remain on balancing volume and revenue with patient outcomes. But in today's constrained reimbursement environment, rehabilitation clinics must be diligent to maximize revenue generation through pricing, volumes, efficiency, and new opportunities.

Alternative Revenue Streams

Rehabilitation services, like traditional physical, occupational, and speech therapies, should be the foundation of any clinic or department. To either increase income or to remain viable, adding revenues from non-rehab sources proves valuable. Here are some examples of potential alternative revenue streams a rehabilitation clinic could pursue beyond traditional insurance-based services.

Cash-Based Services

Cash-based services are those that do not involve submitting claims to insurance companies. Not submitting claims can be an appropriate path for a variety of reasons. Some patients are uninsured and would use a self-pay package for rehab services offered at discounted rates compared to full charges. Insurance does not cover some elective services like nutritional counseling, fitness training, soft tissue massage, injury prevention programs, custom exercise routines, or aquatic therapy; these services work well in a cash-based model.

There are a variety of specific examples of how we might use cash-based services to generate clinic revenue. This list is not exhaustive as there are many other ways to use a cash-based approach to additional revenue sources (e.g., work sites, gyms, fitness studios, senior centers). The key is leveraging therapists' knowledge of anatomy, biomechanics, and exercise prescription to provide customized injury prevention and performance services beyond just rehabilitation.

For Schools

Schools are a great option for cash-based services. The list provided here involves the school paying the clinic or department for the service, but some of these may apply to individual students or families. Here is a list of cash-based services we can provide to schools and school districts.

- Baseline concussion testing for athletes before seasons, then rehab services if concussions occur.

- Athletic training services. This can include the school paying the rehab clinic or department for the service or the clinic can pay the school to offer it, expecting students would use that clinic's rehab services.

- Strength and conditioning programs tailored to different sports teams.

- Educational seminars on injury prevention, nutrition, and hydration for coaches and athletes.

- Training and certification for coaches in emergency procedures, first aid, protective equipment fitting.

- Ergonomic assessments for computer labs and classrooms to prevent repetitive injuries.

For Athletes

Athletes are another ideal group to work with. This group is constantly searching for programming that will help them achieve their goals; rehab professionals are well-suited to provide these services. Examples include:

- Customized conditioning programs based on an athlete's goals, strengths, needs.

- Movement screenings to identify areas prone to injury and address with focused training.

- Video analysis of mechanics during sport motions to improve technique and performance.

- Periodized training plans for in-season maintenance vs. offseason gains.

- Guidance in recovery techniques, nutrition supplementation, and gear selection.

For Adults

Non-injured adults—and even some children—would also benefit from cash-based services provided by rehab clinics.

- Personal training services for those looking to get in shape.

- Group bootcamps and strength classes at various levels.

- Yoga, Pilates, Tai Chi, barre, and balance classes for balance, flexibility, control, and injury prevention.

- Worksite ergonomic consults and stretching/posture guidance to prevent desk job pain.

- Fall prevention classes on balance exercises, gait training, home safety techniques.

All of these are viable options. To begin, conduct surveys with patients and community members to assess their interest in potential class offerings and determine the most suitable schedules. When deciding on new services or classes, the revenue generated from these services must be compared to any potential revenue loss. Though it can be an effective strategy, use caution when using and do not focus on cash-based services at the expense of potentially higher paying patient care services. Some of these services may not generate as much revenue as patient care, but instead they may serve as loss leaders. A **loss leader** in rehab is a service offered at a price below cost, often to attract new patients or encourage them to use more profitable services later. For example, a rehab center might offer a discounted injury prevention program to attract new patients, hoping they will then choose the center's more expensive ongoing physical therapy services. Offering specialty classes provides additional revenue streams while also serving community needs and keeping the clinic top of mind for referrals.

Retail Product Sales

Selling products that are related to rehab and the rehab process is another way to increase clinic and department revenue. Here are some examples of how a rehabilitation clinic could establish retail product sales.

- Set up a physical store within the clinic waiting area to display products.

- Stock common assistive devices like braces, slings, crutches, compression socks. Have fitting samples available.

- Display exercise equipment like resistance bands, dumbbells, pulleys, foam rollers, yoga blocks. Allow patients to touch and demo products.

- Sell branded, prepackaged topical analgesics like Biofreeze® gel or essential oil blends.

- Offer healthy snacks like protein bars, hydration mixes, nuts and trail mixes targeting recovery and nutrition.

To improve the chances of increasing sales, you might display posters, pricing signs, and brochures highlighting the benefits and uses of each product. Train staff on product details so they can educate and sell to patients effectively. Add online ordering via an e-commerce site so existing patients can purchase anytime.

You might also provide purchase incentives like discount bundles, loyalty points, or product trials to drive sales. This works especially well with other cash-based services.

Analyze sales data to identify top selling vs. slow-moving items and adjust inventory accordingly. The goal is providing rehabilitation-focused retail products that add value for patients while also incrementally contributing to clinic revenue and margins.

Grant Funding

Applying for grants and outside funding to support, enhance or expand rehabilitation clinic programming can offset pressures on operational budgets. Dedicating resources to identify and craft quality applications is key to accessing these opportunities.

- Identify government grant programs for healthcare services from sources like HRSA, NIH, CDC, state public health agencies.

- Research foundation and non-profit grant opportunities related to their focus areas, such as from the American Heart Association for cardiac rehab.

- Partner with a community hospital or public health entity if needed to be eligible for certain public grants.

Other Revenue Streams

There are many other ways to increase department revenue. Some examples are:

- Rent space, equipment, or pools to other providers when not in use.

- Education seminars for health professionals needing CEUs.

- Rehabilitation-focused health seminars to local businesses or the community for a fee or as loss leaders.

- Partner with fitness centers, gyms, or training studios to provide rehabilitation expertise and split revenues.

As always, analyze sales, attendance, and customer feedback in order to refine classes and remain relevant. Some of these programs can indeed generate additional revenue, but some may be too burdensome to manage or may cause negative margins.

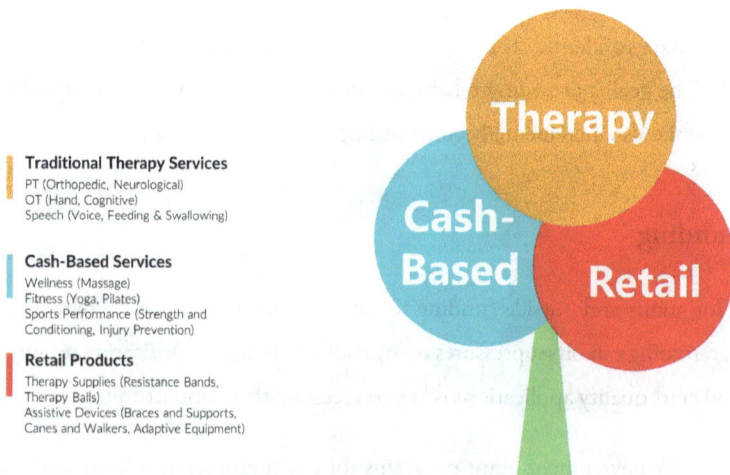

Traditional Therapy Services
PT (Orthopedic, Neurological)
OT (Hand, Cognitive)
Speech (Voice, Feeding & Swallowing)

Cash-Based Services
Wellness (Massage)
Fitness (Yoga, Pilates)
Sports Performance (Strength and
Conditioning, Injury Prevention)

Retail Products
Therapy Supplies (Resistance Bands,
Therapy Balls)
Assistive Devices (Braces and Supports,
Canes and Walkers, Adaptive Equipment)

Revenue Streams for a Rehabilitation Clinic

Exploring and developing multiple revenue streams can help rehab clinics diversify their income sources and enhance financial stability. By offering a wide range of services and products, clinics can attract new patients, meet the evolving needs of their existing clientele, and create additional opportunities for growth and profitability.

Impact of Value-Based Reimbursement on Rehab Revenue Strategies

The healthcare industry's ongoing shift from fee-for-service to value-based reimbursement models is significantly impacting rehab revenue strategies. Value-based models, such as bundled payments, aim to align financial incentives with patient outcomes and care quality, rather than rewarding volume alone. This transformation presents both opportunities and challenges for rehab providers.

Bundled Payments

Bundled payments, also known as episode-based payments, provide a single, fixed reimbursement for all services related to a specific condition or procedure over a defined period. For rehab, this might include a comprehensive payment for a hip replacement episode, covering the surgery, inpatient rehab, outpatient therapy, and related care for 90 days post-discharge.

Opportunities

Care Coordination—Bundled payments encourage greater collaboration and care coordination among providers across the continuum. Rehab professionals have an opportunity to work closely with acute care, post-acute, and outpatient teams to optimize patient transitions and outcomes.

Efficiency Incentives—With a fixed payment for the entire episode, providers are incentivized to deliver care efficiently and minimize unnecessary services or readmissions. Rehab teams can streamline care pathways, standardize best practices, and use resources judiciously.

Quality Improvement—Bundled payments reward providers for achieving better patient outcomes and reducing complications. Rehab leaders can leverage this focus on quality to implement evidence-based protocols, track functional outcomes, and continuously improve care delivery.

Challenges

Financial Risk—Under bundled payments, rehab providers assume greater financial risk. If the cost of care exceeds the fixed reimbursement, the provider bears the loss. This requires careful cost management, case mix analysis, and risk stratification to ensure financial viability.

Data and Analytics—Succeeding with bundled payments demands robust data systems and analytics capabilities. Rehab leaders must be able to track costs, outcomes, and resource utilization across the entire episode to identify opportunities for improvement and negotiate favorable contracts.

Patient Complexity—Bundled payments may not adequately account for variations in patient complexity or socioeconomic factors that can impact rehab outcomes. Risk adjustment methodologies are still evolving, and rehab leaders must advocate for fair reimbursement based on their patient population.

Strategies for Success

To thrive under value-based reimbursement models like bundled payments, rehab leaders should consider the following strategies:

Develop Strategic Partnerships—Collaborate with high-performing acute care, post-acute, and outpatient providers to create integrated care networks that can effectively manage bundled payment episodes.

Invest in Care Redesign—Analyze care processes and implement evidence-based protocols to optimize efficiency, quality, and outcomes across the rehab continuum. Engage frontline staff in continuous improvement efforts.

Enhance Data Capabilities—Invest in robust data systems and analytics tools to track costs, outcomes, and performance metrics. Use this data to inform contract negotiations, resource allocation, and quality improvement initiatives.

Embrace Risk Stratification—Develop risk stratification models to identify high-risk patients and tailor care management strategies accordingly. Explore innovative approaches like telehealth and remote monitoring to support high-need patients cost-effectively.

Educate and Engage Patients—Educate patients about their rehab journey, expected outcomes, and role in self-management. Engage patients and families as active partners in the care process to optimize results and satisfaction under bundled payments.

Value-based reimbursement models like bundled payments are here to stay, and rehab leaders must adapt their revenue strategies accordingly. By focusing on care coordination, efficiency, quality, and data-driven decision-making, rehab providers can successfully navigate this shift and position themselves for long-term sustainability. Embracing these changes proactively will be critical for revenue growth and financial stability in the evolving healthcare landscape.

Conclusion

Pursuing creative revenue generation opportunities beyond traditional insurance can help rehabilitation clinics diversify income streams during times of reimbursement pressure or shifting payer models. The key is aligning offerings with organizational strengths, capabilities, and patients' needs.

As the revenue generation ideas keep flowing, Amanda can't help but feel a sense of excitement. "Who says healthcare has to be all serious all the time?" She's already imagining the look on her patients' faces when they see the new "Yoga for Couch Potatoes" class on the schedule.

Personal Reflection: Amanda realizes that generating revenue is not just about the bottom line; it's about finding creative ways to serve her community and to support her team. She learns the importance of thinking outside the box, taking calculated risks, and involving her staff in the brainstorming process. She commits to keeping an open mind and to always putting patient care first, even as she explores new revenue streams.

Chapter Six

Financial Decision-Making in Rehabilitation

Amanda's faced with a tough decision when the department's trusty old isokinetic machine finally decides to retire to the great physical therapy gym in the sky. She's pretty sure that "cost-benefit analysis" doesn't mean weighing the pros and cons of buying a shiny new machine versus investing in a lifetime supply of bubble wrap for patient safety. In a meeting with the finance director, Allison Johnson, Amanda prepares to crunch some numbers.

"Allison, I need your help. Our isokinetic machine has officially kicked the bucket, and I'm torn between repairing it for the umpteenth time or splurging on a new one that doesn't sound like a dying whale," Amanda sighs, holding up a spreadsheet filled with more question marks than a mystery novel.

Allison smiles, "Ah, the eternal question: to repair or to replace? Let's break down the costs and benefits of each option and see which one makes the most sense for our patients and our bottom line."

Together, they dive into the data, weighing factors like efficiency, patient outcomes, and long-term cost savings. Amanda even suggests a third option: teaching patients to walk like penguins to avoid the need for gait analysis altogether. In the end, they make a data-driven decision that balances financial responsibility with patient care.

E ffective financial decision-making is critical for the success of any rehabilitation clinic or department. Leaders must regularly evaluate investments, expenditures, and opportunities to ensure the financial health and sustainability of rehabilitation services. This chapter summarizes key financial analysis techniques that can inform major decisions in rehabilitation settings.

Cost-Benefit Analysis

Cost-benefit analysis is a systematic process for calculating and comparing the costs and benefits associated with different decision alternatives. This analysis can help leaders determine if the benefits of a potential investment or expenditure outweigh the costs.

To conduct a cost-benefit analysis, first compile a comprehensive list of the costs associated with each alternative over the full lifetime of the decision. Costs may include initial purchase prices, installation and implementation costs, operating costs, maintenance and upgrade costs, training costs, and any other expenses related to each option. Next, estimate the financial and non-financial benefits of each alternative. Financial benefits may include increased revenue, cost savings, or improved productivity. Non-financial benefits could include things like improved quality of care, better patient or staff satisfaction, reduced risks, and more.

With the costs and benefits enumerated, compare the alternatives. Calculate the net present value of the incremental costs and incremental benefits of one option over another to determine which has the highest value. The option with the highest net benefit is generally the best financial decision. However, non-financial factors also deserve consideration in the decision-making process.

Cost-benefit analysis has many applications in rehabilitation settings. For example, departments may use it when:

- Evaluating a potential new capital purchase like updated therapy equipment or an electronic medical record system

- Deciding whether to lease or buy a building space

- Determining the ROI of a new staff training program

- Assessing the trade-offs of outsourcing vs. in-sourcing a service line

- Comparing the costs and benefits of adding a new program or service

While cost-benefit analysis provides a logical system for decision-making, leaders should keep some limitations in mind. Accurately projecting costs and benefits over the long term can be difficult. It also requires assigning financial values to intangible benefits. Even with thorough research and estimates, uncertainty is inherent in predicting the future. Therefore, cost-benefit analysis should inform leaders rather than definitively dictate decisions.

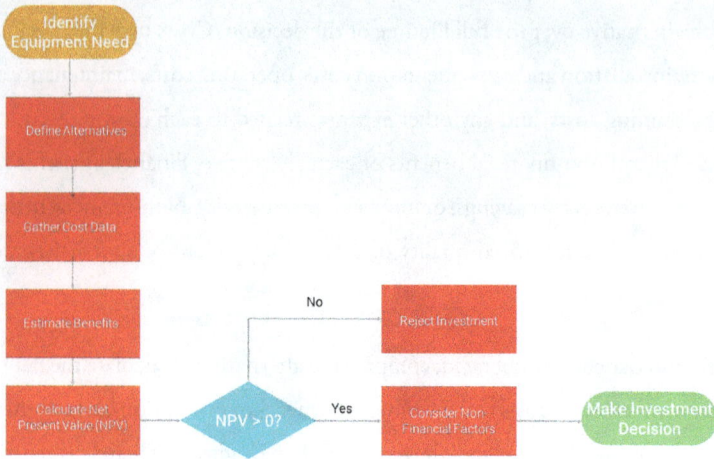

Cost-Benefit Analysis Decision Tree for New Equipment Purchase. Visual representation of the key steps and decision points involved in conducting a cost-benefit analysis for a new equipment purchase in a rehabilitation setting.

Breakeven Analysis

A **breakeven analysis** calculates the quantity of services a rehabilitation clinic or department must provide to cover its fixed costs. The volume identified indicates the "break-even point" where revenues exceed total expenses and begin generating profit.

Conducting a breakeven analysis involves three key steps:

1. Determine the clinic's fixed costs (e.g., rent, utilities, salaries, etc.) for the period of analysis.

2. Determine the clinic's variable costs per unit of service provided. This may include direct labor, supplies, patient consumables, and other expenses that fluctuate with service volume.

3. Divide the total fixed costs by the variable costs per unit to calculate the required volume to breakeven.

For example:

A clinic's monthly fixed operating costs total $100,000 and the variable cost per physical therapy visit averages $50.

$$Breakeven\ Volume = \frac{Fixed\ Costs}{Variable\ Cost\ per\ Unit}$$

$$= \frac{\$100{,}000}{\$50\ per\ visit}$$

$$= 2{,}000\ visits\ per\ month$$

In this example, the clinic must see at least 2,000 visits monthly to generate enough revenue to cover its fixed and variable expenses. Volumes above 2,000 visits will yield increasing profit.

Leaders can use breakeven analysis to determine minimum billing volumes for profitability, set performance targets, and optimize staffing. It provides an important metric for financial discipline and sustainability. Clinics should factor seasonality into breakeven calculations, as patient volumes often fluctuate. It also helps to revisit the analysis periodically to account for changes in costs. While simple in concept, breakeven analysis provides an essential baseline for fiscal stewardship.

Differential Cost Analysis

Differential cost analysis involves evaluating the varying costs between different choices. It enables rehabilitation leaders to filter out sunk costs and non-differential expenses to focus decisions on the costs that truly matter.

A **sunk cost** is an expense incurred in the past that we cannot recover. These costs are irrelevant to future financial decisions because the money has already been spent and cannot be retrieved.

Here's an example:

A physical therapy clinic invests in a new unloading treadmill for $20,000. Regardless of how much revenue the treadmill generates in the future, the initial $20,000 cost is a sunk cost. The clinic should not consider this sunk cost when deciding about future equipment purchases or service pricing.

To perform a differential cost analysis, use these four steps:

1. List all potential costs associated with each decision alternative.

2. Eliminate any sunk costs that have already been incurred and cannot be recovered. These are irrelevant to the decision.

3. Eliminate any costs that are identical across all alternatives. Only differential costs impact the decision.

4. Evaluate the remaining differential costs to determine the best option based on the cost differences.

For example, consider a clinic evaluating whether to purchase updated rehabilitation gym equipment. The analysis can exclude sunk costs, such as the cost of the old equipment and construction expenses for the gym. Since non-differential costs like gym rent and therapist salaries remain fixed regardless of the equipment decision, we can eliminate them as well. The differential cost analysis would focus only on the different potential equipment purchase, delivery, installation, maintenance, and training costs across the options. Comparing only these relevant differential costs simplifies the analysis and provides clearer cost information to guide the equipment acquisition decision.

Common applications of differential cost analysis in rehabilitation settings include:

- Equipment purchasing decisions

- Lease vs. buy analyses

- Make vs. buy analyses for supplies and services

- New program development decisions

- Staffing mix optimizations

- Profitability analyses by service line

By filtering out sunk costs and non-differential items, leaders can distill the decision down to just the costs that truly differ across the alternatives being considered. This sharpens the focus on what matters most in the decision-making process.

Incorporating Qualitative Factors

While the financial analysis techniques covered in this chapter provide critical data to guide decision-making, leaders should also incorporate qualitative factors into the decision-making process. Patient care quality, safety, staff engagement, legal risks, alignment with organizational values and many other intangible considerations can influence a decision. Wise leaders use financial analysis to inform decisions, not dictate them. We need to combine quantifiable cost and profitability data with thoughtful consideration of qualitative factors for balanced decision-making.

Financial discipline and stewardship are imperative for rehabilitation clinics and departments to advance their mission. Methods like cost-benefit analysis, breakeven analysis, and differential cost analysis provide data-driven frameworks to guide major investment and expenditure decisions. When coupled with a consideration of qualitative factors, these techniques allow leaders to make judicious financial decisions positioned for organizational success.

As Amanda and Allison wrap up their cost-benefit analysis, she can't help but feel a sense of accomplishment. "Who knew that making tough decisions could be so rewarding?" she thinks, already planning her next data-driven adventure.

Personal Reflection: Amanda realizes that financial decision-making is not just about the numbers; it's about weighing the impact on

patient care, staff satisfaction, and long-term
sustainability. She learns the importance of
gathering data, considering multiple perspec-
tives, and communicating the rationale behind her choices. She commits to making
transparent, ethical decisions that align with
her department's mission and values.

Chapter Seven

Asset Management in Rehabilitation Settings

Amanda's on a mission to whip the department's assets into shape, and she's armed with a clipboard and a determination to make every piece of equipment last longer than a Twinkie. She's pretty sure that "asset management" doesn't mean teaching the therapy bands to do circus tricks, but she's ready to take on the challenge. In a meeting with the equipment technician, Michael Thompson, Amanda prepares to unleash her inner neat freak.

"Michael, I've been taking an inventory of our equipment, and I think it's time we had a little heart-to-heart with our therapy mats about their job performance," Amanda jokes, hold-

ing up a checklist that's longer than a grocery
store receipt.

Michael chuckles, "Well, I'm pretty sure the
mats are doing their best, but I see your
point. Let's talk about how we can optimize
our equipment maintenance and replacement
schedule to keep everything in tip-top shape."

Together, they develop a plan to track equipment usage, perform regular preventive maintenance, and replace outdated items before
they become a liability. Amanda even suggests
a "Most Valuable Equipment" award to recognize the hardest-working machines in the
department.

Asset management involves tracking, maintaining, and optimizing the equipment,
property, technology, and other fixed assets that enable the delivery of care. Effective asset management is crucial for rehabilitation clinics and departments to maximize
the useful lifespan of assets, reduce costs, and strategically reinvest in key capital needs.
This chapter provides an overview of asset management principles and strategies for
rehabilitation leaders.

Depreciation Basics

Understanding depreciation is fundamental to asset management. **Depreciation** is the
method of allocating the cost of a fixed asset over its useful life. As we use an asset like
equipment, its value diminishes through wear and tear. Organizations can systematically

distribute the loss in value of an asset as an operating expense over each year of its lifespan through depreciation.

Year	Beginning Book Value	Depreciation Expense	Accumulated Depreciation	Ending Book Value
1	$15,000	$2,700	$2,700	$12,300
2	$12,300	$2,700	$5,400	$9,600
3	$9,600	$2,700	$8,100	$6,900
4	$6,900	$2,700	$10,800	$4,200
5	$4,200	$2,700	$13,500	$1,500

Depreciation Schedule for Rehabilitation Equipment. The straight-line depreciation method spreads the depreciable cost of the equipment evenly over its 5-year useful life. The annual depreciation expense remains constant at $2,700, gradually reducing the book value of the equipment until it reaches its salvage value of $1,500 at the end of Year 5.

Assumptions

Equipment: Treadmill

Cost: $15,000

Useful Life: 5 Years

Depreciation Method: Straight-Line

Salvage Value: $1,500

This is right below the figure.

The depreciation expense is calculated using the straight-line method:

$(Cost - Salvage\ Value) \div Useful\ Life$
 $= (\$15,000 - \$1,500) \div 5$
 $= \$2,700\ per\ year$

There are several important details about depreciation.

- Depreciation is a non-cash expense. It does not involve actively paying out funds each year.

- The annual depreciation expense is used to accumulate a contra asset account, called accumulated depreciation. This contra account has a credit balance that increases over time to offset the original asset account.

- By the end of an asset's useful life, its original cost will be fully depreciated. The asset account and accumulated depreciation account will net to zero on the balance sheet.

- Organizations may depreciate assets using different methods, such as straight-line, double declining balance, and units of production. Straight-line is most common and spreads depreciation evenly across each year.

- Depreciation lowers net income on financial statements. But it provides organizations a tax deduction since it is counted as a business expense.

A **contra asset account** is a special type of asset account that has a *credit balance* (negative balance) instead of the usual debit balance associated with asset accounts. It exists to *offset the value of a related asset account,* providing a more accurate picture of the net value of the asset.

Contra asset accounts reduce the *carrying value* (recorded value) of a specific asset on the balance sheet. Doing this provides a more *realistic representation* of the asset's true worth by accounting for depreciation, valuation adjustments, or other factors that decrease its value.

Some examples include:

Accumulated Depreciation: This is the most common contra asset account. It tracks the total depreciation expense recorded for a fixed asset (e.g., equipment, buildings) over time, reducing its book value on the balance sheet.

Allowance for Doubtful Accounts: This contra asset account reflects the estimated amount of accounts receivable that may not be collected due to bad debts. It reduces the value of the accounts receivable account on the balance sheet.

Reserve for Obsolescence: This contra asset account reflects a potential reduction in value due to technological advancements or changing market conditions. It reduces the book value of an asset on the balance sheet.

Why Use Contra Asset Accounts?

Using contra asset accounts provides a clearer picture of an asset's actual value by considering factors that decrease its worth. It also separates these reductions from the main asset account and allows for better financial analysis and understanding of asset valuation.

Contra asset accounts are essential bookkeeping tools that ensure the financial statements accurately reflect the net realizable value of assets, providing a more accurate picture of a company's financial health.

For rehabilitation departments, some common depreciable assets include therapy equipment, furniture, computers, software, vehicles, and leasehold improvements made to rented building spaces. Tracking depreciation schedules helps leaders understand when assets may need replacement and informs capital planning.

Preventive Maintenance

Preventive maintenance involves routinely inspecting and servicing assets to minimize breakdowns and maximize operational life. For rehabilitation equipment, developing a comprehensive preventive maintenance program is essential. Key aspects include:

- Maintaining a fixed asset inventory to track all significant equipment. This should include details like model number, serial number, purchase date, and warranty/service contract info.

- Adhering to all manufacturer recommended maintenance for each asset. This may involve tasks like lubrication, calibration, inspections, part replacements, software updates, and safety checks on a defined schedule.

- Training in-house staff or contracting vendors to complete maintenance tasks. Clinical engineers can provide specialized biomedical equipment services.

- Scheduling regular maintenance during downtimes to minimize clinical disruptions.

- Recording all maintenance procedures performed on each asset. Software solutions can track maintenance history.

- Monitoring assets for performance issues and diagnosing problems early.

Preventive maintenance requires diligence and planning, but significantly extends the usable life of assets. It also reduces unplanned downtime that can negatively impact clinic operations and patient care.

Capital Replacement Planning

Careful planning must precede asset replacement. Rehabilitation leaders should take a strategic approach by forecasting long-term capital needs based on the ages and conditions of current assets. We must also factor in projected service growth, technology advancements, and obsolescence. It is important to set target replacement cycles for different asset classes (e.g., some rehab equipment should be replaced every 6 to 8 years) and benchmark these targets against industry norms.

In addition, using a phased, realistic timeline for replacements that minimizes disruptions, leaders must prioritize and optimize spending on mission-critical assets that directly impact service delivery and revenue generation. They must also explore alternative financing strategies, like loans, bonds, leases, grants, cash reserves, and philanthropy.

Strategically acquiring and replacing assets requires alignment with organizational goals and continuous environmental scanning. Careful planning mitigates risks of poorly timed purchases and service interruptions because of outdated equipment.

Re-deployment and Disposition

Instead of automatically discarding assets that are retired or replaced, rehabilitation leaders should consider re-deployment opportunities. Equipment that is fully depreciated but still functional may have continued value in other sites of care or for different uses. Leaders can extract additional value from assets by:

- Evaluating assets for re-deployment potential when replacement occurs

- Refurbishing or reconfiguring assets cost-effectively to enable re-use

- Transferring assets to other departments or practice locations with needs

- Repurposing assets for new functions if still operable

- Donating retired assets to charity to earn tax benefits

For assets that we cannot re-deploy, we must properly dispose of them responsibly. Disposal options include selling through auction or salvage companies, recycling, or safe hazardous waste disposal. Proper disposal removes risks associated with non-functioning equipment and may offset small replacement costs.

Optimizing Utilization

Utilization refers to the percentage of total available time that fixed assets are operational and productive. High utilization indicates assets are generating maximal value. Under-utilization wastes potential capacity. Rehabilitation leaders should track and optimize asset utilization by performing the following tasks.

- Monitoring usage schedules, downtime, patient volume, and other utilization metrics

- Identifying bottlenecks where staff, space, or equipment limitations constrain utilization

- Right-sizing assets based on realistic demand projections to avoid over-capacity

- Cross-training staff on equipment to improve scheduling flexibility

- Exploring alternate uses during downtime (e.g., community classes in gym space)

- Comparing utilization trends across different locations or service lines

- Adjusting staffing levels, treatment space, and asset quantities to maximize utilization

Proactively optimizing asset utilization reduces waste and improves the return on capital investments while also boosting overall clinic productivity.

Outsourcing Considerations

Some asset management functions, like maintenance, capital planning, and disposal, may be effectively outsourced to specialized vendors. Benefits of outsourcing can include cost savings, improved efficiency, access to technical expertise, and risk transfer. When considering outsourcing options, leaders should evaluate maintenance agreements with equipment manufacturers or third parties, full-service leasing of major equipment assets, capital planning consultants, auction services for asset recovery and re-sale, and IT management for systems and infrastructure.

However, core assets that provide a competitive advantage or directly impact clinical care are often best kept in-house if adequate expertise exists internally. Outsourcing can help ease resource limitations, but it should be in line with the organization's strategic goals.

Conclusion

Assets are central to service delivery, making asset management a pivotal business responsibility. Leaders must steward assets across their full lifecycle to maximize the value derived. While requiring resource commitments, robust asset management ultimately reduces the total cost of ownership and enables strategic reinvestment. By taking a data-driven, forward-looking approach, rehabilitation organizations can optimize their asset portfolio.

As Amanda and Michael finalize their equipment management plan, she can't help but smile. "Who knew that taking care of our therapy mats could be so fulfilling?" she muses, already drafting a heartfelt thank-you note to the hardest-working treadmill in the department.

Personal Reflection: Amanda realizes that asset management is not just about maintaining equipment; it's about being a good steward of the resources entrusted to her. She learns the importance of preventive maintenance, data-driven decision-making, and involving her team in the process. She commits to treating her department's assets with the same care and respect she shows her patients and staff.

Chapter Eight

Financing Strategies for Capital Needs in Rehabilitation

Amanda's got big dreams for the department, but she knows that dreams don't come cheap. She's knows that "capital investment" doesn't mean buying a giant inflatable bouncy castle for the therapy gym, but she's ready to explore all other options. In a meeting with the hospital's CFO, Jonah Edwards, Amanda prepares to put on her best "serious business" face.

"Jonah, I've got some exciting ideas for expanding our services and upgrading our facilities, but I'm pretty sure I can't just sell lemonade in the parking lot to fund them," Amanda grins, holding up a proposal that's more colorful than a box of crayons.

Jonah laughs, "Well, I admire your enthusiasm, but you're right. We need to be strategic about how we finance these projects. Let's talk about some options, like grants, fundraising, and maybe even a bake sale or two."

Together, they explore a range of financing strategies, from philanthropic donations to low-interest loans. Amanda even suggests a "Sponsor a Therapy Dog" program, where donors can help fund the department's furry ambassadors of healing. In the end, they develop a comprehensive plan that balances innovation with financial stability.

Accessing capital is necessary for rehabilitation clinics and practices to fund large investments in facilities, equipment, technologies, and other strategic initiatives. This chapter explores common financing strategies used in rehabilitation settings, securing financing, and key considerations for developing an optimal capital structure.

Capital Financing Strategies

Several core options exist to finance major capital expenditures. **Funded Depreciation** involves setting aside estimated depreciation dollars each year to self-fund upcoming replacement needs. **Philanthropy** efforts secure donations, grants, sponsorships from individuals, foundations, corporations, and government entities to fund capital projects. This works best for larger initiatives with community benefits. **Debt Financing** allows organizations to borrow funds that are repaid over time with interest through instruments like loans, bonds, and leases. Many organizations commonly use this method, but it also adds liability. **Operating Surpluses** involves allocating excess revenues over expenses to fund capital needs. This first requires consistently generating positive margins. **Equity** use means organizations sell ownership shares in the organization in return for capital, typically used by for-profit entities. Equity relinquishes control and ownership.

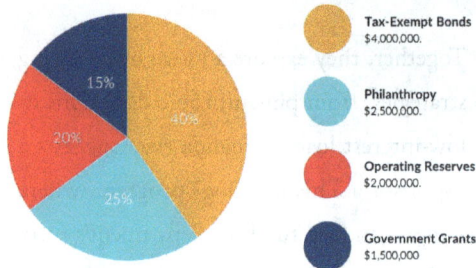

Capital Project Funding Sources. Funding Mix for Rehabilitation Center Expansion Project. Total Project Cost: $10 Million.

The optimal mix of these funding sources depends on the rehabilitation provider's circumstances. Non-profit and government providers have limitations on equity and retained earnings that for-profits do not face. The sections below explore debt financing and philanthropy in greater detail given their prominence in capital acquisition for rehabilitation facilities.

Debt Financing

Taking on debt through loans or bonds is likely the most common avenue for financing major capital projects in rehabilitation. By adopting this approach, organizations can secure significant amounts of capital that would otherwise be unattainable through existing operational cash flows, all while spreading out the repayment obligations over an extended duration. Financing in this way means groups can take full advantage of capital immediately to accelerate projects while potentially deducting interest expenses to reduce taxable income.

Debt also carries risks, however. Debt requires regular payments that add to expenses and cash flow burden; failure to pay resulting in default consequences and its use increases overall organizational risk through leverage.

Two primary debt instruments used are bonds and loans, though other options exist.

Bonds

Issuing a bond enables capital to be raised from investors in exchange for a fixed return paid as interest over a defined term until the principal is repaid. Government entities commonly issue bonds, but non-profit rehabilitation providers also use them to fund major facility and equipment projects. If tax-exempt, bond interest is not taxed at issuance or when received by investors. This provides capital at lower costs due to the tax advantages. Bond interest rates depend on the perceived risk of the issuing organization based on financial health and credit ratings.

Loans

Loans provide capital repaid with interest based on terms negotiated with banks or other lending institutions. This is a simple financing method but often comes with higher interest rates and faster repayment terms compared to bonds. Loans may be secured by specific assets, like property or equipment.

Other

Other debt financing options include:

- Leasing rather than purchasing assets, avoiding large upfront costs

- Hospital partnerships where capital is provided in exchange for revenue sharing

- Mortgaging real estate to access equity for other capital uses

- Vendor financing packages for major equipment acquisitions

- Government programs like HUD loans or the USDA Community Facilities program

When using debt, it is critical to borrow only what is reasonably affordable based on projected operating cash flows. Too much debt threatens financial sustainability. Conservative debt guidelines for rehabilitation providers are 2-4x debt to earnings and maximum debt service coverage of 20-30% of revenues.

Philanthropy

Seeking donor, grant, or sponsorship funding for capital projects is a key strategy, especially for non-profit rehabilitation providers. Philanthropy offers several advantages, such as no repayment or collateral, improved community engagement, promotion of the organization's mission and vision, and establishing new relationships with donors.

There are several common approaches to philanthropy. Some of these tactics include:

- *Naming rights*—Attaching a donor's name to a facility, department, or equipment in exchange for a donation. This provides meaningful recognition opportunities.

- *Targeted campaigns*—Marketing campaigns promoting a specific capital cause that donors can support, like a new pediatric gym or prosthetic lab.

- *Grants*—Applying for grant funding from private foundations, corporations, and government sources by tying requests to their capital priorities.

- *Events*—Fundraisers such as galas or golf tournaments where a portion of proceeds go towards capital initiatives. This engages the community while raising funds.

- *Major gifts*—Approaching individual major donors capable of transformative gifts of perhaps $1 million or more to support large projects.

- *Planned giving*—Stewarding bequests and gifts through wills, life insurance trusts, donor advised funds, and other planned gifts vehicles.

Successful capital philanthropy requires building a pipeline of donor prospects, making compelling requests, and recognizing donors' contributions. While not sufficient alone, philanthropy can substantially complement other financing sources for rehabilitation facilities.

Obtaining Financing

The process of securing external financing for major capital projects involves several key steps:

1. *Analyzing capital needs and financing options*—Determine the scope and specifics of the initiatives to be funded. Estimate costs and evaluate potential funding sources.

2. *Reviewing organizational finances*—Assess the current financial health and performance of the organization, including profitability, liquidity, leverage, and key financial ratios. These factors influence lenders.

3. *Obtaining a credit rating (for bonds)*—Crediting rating agencies like Moody's and S&P assign ratings to organizations that indicate creditworthiness and default risk. Higher ratings mean lower interest costs.

4. *Preparing a loan or bond proposal*—Quantify the amount of financing desired, proposed terms, business case, and use of funds. Provide financial statements and organizational details.

5. *Submitting the proposal*—Approach banks/lending institutions for loans or engage an investment bank to structure and sell a bond issuance.

6. *Negotiating terms*—Loan interest rates and bond yields are negotiated based on prevailing markets, the organization's risk profile and credit ratings, collateral or security provided, and overall demand.

7. *Closing and receiving funds*—Finalize all legal documentation and agreements to close the financing. After closing, the parties receive the funds according to the negotiated terms.

The more financially sound the rehabilitation organization, the better options it will have in securing affordable capital.

Developing an Optimal Capital Structure

When funding capital needs, rehabilitation leaders should pursue a balanced capital structure using a thoughtful mix of financing sources, as an over-reliance on any single source is risky. The ideal blend uses each source in proportion to its advantages and acquisition feasibility for the organization. Specific weights depend on factors like legal structure, revenue size, credit profile, and capital needs.

Non-profit and government rehabilitation providers should emphasize a mix of philanthropy, tax-exempt debt, and funded depreciation reserves to support their capital structure. Overcoming limited access to equity markets involves cultivating donor and community relationships. For-profit providers have more flexibility using retained earnings and equity but can still leverage debt and other options.

A balanced approach creates organizational stability by diversifying the capital structure across multiple accessible sources. Blending financing options also allows for greater capital availability to support growth and expansion goals.

Conclusion

Accessing sufficient capital is a key enabler for rehabilitation providers to modernize facilities, adopt technology, replace equipment, and expand services. While organizational financing options differ based on legal structure, the overall aim of funding strategic investments in a cost-effective manner remains constant. Leaders must pursue a tailored capital mix that optimizes access to capital while maintaining financial health. A balanced capital structure positions rehabilitation organizations for stability and growth.

As Amanda and Jonah wrap up their financing strategy session, she can't help but feel a sense of pride. "Who knew that finding money could be so much fun?" she grins, already brainstorming catchy slogans for the "Sponsor a Therapy Dog" program.

Personal Reflection: Amanda realizes that financing is not just about securing funds; it's about building relationships and telling a compelling story. She learns the importance of aligning her funding requests with the hospital's mission, involving stakeholders in the process, and thinking creatively about potential sources of support. She commits to being a responsible steward of the resources she secures and to always putting patient care first.

Chapter Nine

Managing the Supply Chain in Rehabilitation Clinics

Amanda's on a quest to tame the wild world of supply chain management, and she's armed with a spreadsheet and a determination to make every penny count. She's pretty sure that "supply chain optimization" doesn't mean teaching the therapy bands to form a conga line, but she's ready to learn. In a meeting with the supply chain manager, Gen Hamilton, Amanda prepares to unleash her inner bargain hunter.

"Gen, I've been looking at our supply costs, and I think it's time we had a little chat about our relationship with foam rollers," Amanda

smirks, holding up a report that's more highlighter than white space.

Gen laughs, "I hear you, Amanda. It's easy
to get carried away with the fun colors and
patterns, but let's talk about how we can
streamline our ordering process and find some
cost-saving opportunities."

Together, they explore strategies like partnering with group purchasing organizations,
standardizing inventory, and implementing
just-in-time ordering. Amanda even suggests a
"Supply Chain Superhero" award for the staff
member who comes up with the most creative
cost-saving idea.

The supply chain encompasses the flow of goods and services from manufacturers and suppliers to the end providers. Effective supply chain management is important for rehabilitation clinics and departments to ensure consistent availability of necessary supplies and equipment. This chapter explores supply chain fundamentals, best practices, and strategies to optimize supply expenses and clinical operations.

Components of the Rehabilitation Supply Chain

There are several key entities that make up the typical rehabilitation clinic supply chain. Each included entity has a specific role to play in the process.

Suppliers and Manufacturers

Companies that produce the wide range of medical supplies, devices, equipment, and other products used in rehabilitation care delivery are suppliers or manufacturers. Gloves, wound dressings, therapy equipment, and assistive devices are sourced from manufacturers and distributors specializing in these products.

Group Purchasing Organizations

Group purchasing organizations—GPOs—aggregate purchasing volume for member healthcare organizations. They negotiate discounted pricing contracts with manufacturers and provide access to a network of supplies. Using a GPO leverages economies of scale.

Distribution Centers and Wholesalers

Warehouses and logistics companies that receive, store, and distribute supplies are referred to as distribution centers or wholesalers. They offer rehab groups efficient order fulfillment and inventory management.

Delivery Services

Delivery services are transportation providers that facilitate the physical movement of supplies and equipment via shipping networks. The focus here is on timely, reliable delivery of supplies and equipment.

Clinics and Therapists

The care providers that ultimately use the supplied products and equipment with patients are the clinics and therapists themselves. It is their supply needs that determine demand.

While linear in concept, an intricate, interconnected supply web underlies rehabilitation operations. Breakdowns anywhere along the chain disrupt clinical workflows and care quality.

Effective Supply Chain Attributes

High-performing supply chains that optimize costs and clinical operations help ensure efficient operations. These supply chains exhibit several key attributes.

Low Inventory Costs

Lean inventory management reduces expenses related to storage, handling, insurance, taxes, obsolescence, and spoilage. Lean principles include standardizing supplies, maintaining **just-in-time** stock levels, and eliminating waste.

Rapid Fulfillment

Delivering supplies and equipment to facilities in a timely manner is necessary to avoid backorders and shortages. This requires excellent forecasting, supplier collaboration, and logistics.

Purchasing Power

GPO contracts and consolidated buying volume provide leverage to negotiate better supplier pricing and terms. This lowers total supply costs.

Data Integration

Supply chain data, like inventory levels, usage trends, and purchase orders, are integrated across providers, GPOs, distributors, and manufacturers for efficiency.

Transparency

Supply chain partners provide visibility of procurement costs, clinical outcomes associated with supplies, and performance metrics through advanced reporting. This enables continuous improvement.

Backup Systems

Contingency plans for supply disruptions or backlogs maintain continuity of operations. This includes alternate suppliers, substitutes, and inventory buffers.

Achieving these attributes requires actively managing every link in the supply chain. Strong processes and relationships better connect supplies to patient needs.

Key Supply Chain Processes

Optimizing rehabilitation supply chain operations involves focusing on several key processes.

1. *Needs Assessment*—Regularly review supply needs with clinicians and therapists. Analyze item usage, costs, and alternatives. Identify opportunities to standardize items used across programs.

2. *Sourcing and Procurement*—Use GPO contracts and competitive bidding to select reliable vendors with quality products at low prices. Consolidate purchases with fewer suppliers when possible for added leverage.

3. *Inventory Management*—Determine par stock levels for each item that provides buffers without excess. Monitor perpetual inventory digitally as supplies are consumed. Replenish based on set reorder points.

4. *Logistics and Delivery*—Schedule and track incoming supply deliveries. Verify shipments for accuracy and quality. Secure climate-controlled storage areas to protect inventory.

5. *Accounts Payable*—Match receipts to supplier invoices to validate charges. Take prompt payment discounts when offered. Processing invoices quickly improves cash flow for suppliers, which may incentivize pricing.

6. *Waste Reduction*—Eliminate outdated, unused supplies from inventory through "first in, first out" tracking. Repurpose or donate beneficial items when possible.

7. *Data Analysis*—Aggregate supply chain data on costs, inventory turnover, and

supplier performance metrics. Analyze trends to identify optimization opportunities.

Small inefficiencies in any of these areas can significantly affect costs and clinical operations over time. A value analysis approach and continuous improvement mentality can yield major supply chain advances.

Strategic Sourcing

More rehabilitation departments are pursuing strategic sourcing initiatives to better leverage their purchasing power. This goes beyond the tactical process of procuring supplies to take a strategic approach to the entire supplier market. Key components include:

- analyzing total annual expenditure by supply category and identifying the top cost categories with the most leverage potential. For example, durable medical equipment may represent a large portion of total spending,

- assessing the supplier marketplace for each key category, noting major vendors, their capabilities, strengths, and weaknesses. Determine the optimal number of suppliers to cultivate,

- developing data-driven scorecards for incumbent supplier performance tracking metrics like product quality, fulfillment rates, pricing trends, and support responsiveness,

- using scorecard data to inform competitive bidding processes and requests for proposals to select preferred suppliers based on performance and value,

- negotiating strategic long-term contracts with chosen suppliers using collective bargaining power. Securing lower pricing in exchange for loyalty and volume commitments, and

- continuously monitoring contract adherence and expanding business with top-performing vendors.

This level of active engagement with the supplier market rather than passive purchasing reduces supply expense while supporting clinical excellence.

Inventory Optimization

Inventory carries costs related to storage, spoilage, taxes, insurance, and obsolescence. The *Economic Order Quantity (EOQ)* **formula** determines the ideal order size that minimizes total inventory holding and replenishment costs. It evaluates the trade-off between order size and frequency.

While EOQ provides a helpful starting point, other factors also merit consideration when defining *par stock levels*. Usage patterns may fluctuate seasonally, for example. Slow-moving supplies may warrant lower minimum quantities to avoid waste from expiration. In contrast, specialty supplies difficult to source quickly merit deeper reserves. Inventory optimization is ultimately a balancing act requiring data, experience, and judgement.

Technology Enablers

Advances like barcode scanning, electronic data interchange, robotics, and inventory management software are transforming rehabilitation supply chain capabilities. Some emerging technologies offer major potential benefits.

- Predictive analytics to forecast supply demand more accurately using clinical datasets and machine learning algorithms. This smoothes inventory flows.

- RFID tagging of supplies to enable real-time tracking and perpetual inventory visibility as items move through the supply chain.

- Automated inventory replenishment based on smart barcode scanning and pre-set par levels. This reduces **stockouts**.

- clouID-based services offer cloud computing solutions that allow suppliers real-time access to a provider's inventory data, enabling them to anticipate and fulfill restocking needs proactively, thus optimizing inventory levels and minimizing stockouts or overstocking.

While representing cost outlays, these supply chain technologies can readily yield a strong **return on investment—ROI**—through efficiency gains, lower inventories, and better clinical operations.

Conclusion

Fluid supply chain operations enable rehabilitation therapists to deliver care without disruption. Leaders must take a strategic approach to managing each component of their supply chain for optimal efficiency and costs. Leveraging purchasing power, maximizing technologies, mining data, and collaborating across suppliers allows rehabilitation clinics to ensure reliable access to the vital supplies that underpin patient outcomes and experience.

As Amanda and Gen wrap up their supply chain optimization plan, she can't help but feel a sense of satisfaction. "Who knew that streamlining inventory could be so exciting?" she muses, already planning a "Supply Chain Superhero" themed party for her team.

Personal Reflection: Amanda realizes that supply chain management is not just about ordering products; it's about ensuring that her team has the tools they need to provide the best possible care. She learns the importance of data-driven decision-making, collaboration with suppliers, and involving her staff in the process. She commits to being a responsible steward of her department's resources and to always putting patient outcomes first.

Chapter Ten

Revenue Cycle Management in Rehabilitation Settings

Amanda's determined to make the revenue cycle go 'round, and she's armed with a flowchart and a can-do attitude. She's pretty sure that "revenue cycle management" doesn't mean riding a unicycle while juggling insurance claims, but she's ready to take on the challenge. In a meeting with the revenue cycle manager, Max Brown, Amanda prepares to channel her inner detective.

"Max, I've been investigating our claims data, and I think we might have a case of the mysterious disappearing reimbursements," Amanda quips, holding up a stack of denied claims that's taller than a toddler.

Max laughs. "Well, let's put on our deerstalker
hats and get to the bottom of this mystery.
We'll leave no stone unturned, or in this case,
no claim unexamined!"

Together, they dive into the world of coding,
documentation, and insurance verification,
determined to solve the case of the vanishing
payments. Amanda even suggests a "Revenue
Cycle Detective" badge for the staff member
who cracks the toughest claim denial.

T he revenue cycle encompasses all administrative and clinical activities that generate
   revenue from patient care. Revenue cycle management maximizes reimbursement
while maintaining compliance and positive patient financial experiences. This chapter
explores the core components of the revenue cycle and strategies for rehabilitation clinics
to optimize their revenue management processes.

Revenue Cycle Components

The revenue cycle flows through several interconnected components, each playing a
crucial role in ensuring the smooth and efficient capture, billing, and collection of revenue for rehabilitation services. These components work together to minimize revenue
leakage, optimize reimbursement, and maintain the financial health of the organization.
Understanding the function and importance of each component is essential for effective
revenue cycle management.

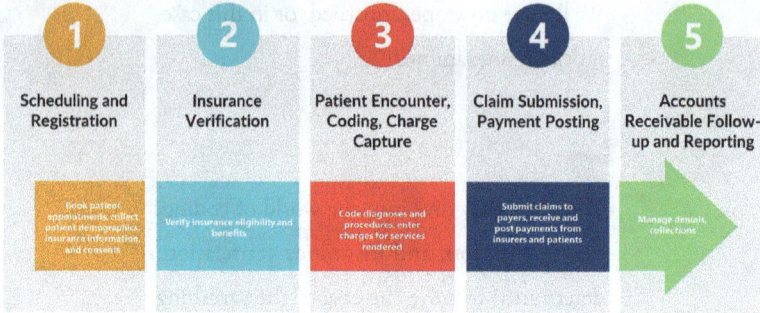

Rehabilitation Revenue Cycle Management Process. Key components and workflows of the revenue cycle process for rehabilitation.

Scheduling

Successfully booking patient appointments to ensure access and capacity utilization. Efficient schedules fill therapist's time.

Registration

Collecting complete patient demographics, insurance information, authorizations, and payments at check-in. This prevents billing rejections.

Clinical

Documenting all diagnoses, interventions, equipment, supplies, and minutes to support billing charges.

Coding

Assigning standardized codes to clinical documentation that provide insights into patient complexity, services rendered, and medical necessity. Proper coding is crucial for reimbursement.

Charge Capture

Entering charges for each billable item and service into the billing system during or directly after care delivery. Missed charges negatively impact revenue.

Claim Submission

Transmitting claims with appropriate codes and documentation to payers within timely filing deadlines.

Payment Posting

Applying received payments to open encounters and patient accounts. Timely posting prevents revenue leaks.

Denial Management

Identifying, researching, and appealing any unjustified claim denials through payer resubmission or reconsideration processes. Preventing denials boosts revenue realization.

Collections

Pursuing unpaid balances through statements, calls, negotiations, and other avenues to collect owed amounts from patients and payers. Uncollected debt erodes revenue.

While presented sequentially, these processes contain interdependencies and bottlenecks that rehab leaders must proactively manage. For example, incomplete clinical documentation leads to inaccurate coding, which prompts payment denials and hinders collections. A holistic view of revenue cycle workflows is necessary to maximize performance.

Revenue Cycle Best Practices

There are several strategies and considerations to optimize rehabilitation clinic revenue cycles. Embedding these practices into the patient's experience and encounter will help to ensure proper, timely payment.

- Integrating EHR and billing systems to reduce manual data entry and speed claim generation with accurate codes.

- Monitoring claim rejections rates, denial reasons, and payer metrics. Use data to identify and address problem areas.

- Studying metrics like days in A/R and net collection percentage to find bottlenecks in the cycle.

- Establishing patient financial responsibility estimates upfront during scheduling. Collect pre-service payments when possible.

- Training front desk staff on verification of eligibility, benefits, authorizations, and payer requirements to prevent claims issues.

- Instituting medical necessity checks for ordered therapies to confirm payer coverage.

- Performing insurance pre-authorization and concurrent reviews to validate reimbursement.

- Developing provider incentives based on productivity, quality, compliance, and other value dimensions.

- Outsourcing revenue cycle functions like coding, billing, and collections to specialized partners when advantageous.

- Using automated work queues and reminders to ensure claim follow-up and denial appeals.

- Establishing a culture focused on revenue integrity, compliance, efficiency, and patient satisfaction.

While people, processes, and technologies all play key roles, sound revenue cycle operations require the right underlying mentality. Leaders must ingrain revenue excellence as a core priority across rehabilitation departments.

Improving Front-End Revenue Cycle Operations

The front-end revenue cycle components of scheduling, registration, documentation, and coding set the trajectory for the entire downstream cycle. When done well, they significantly boost realization and reduce costly rework. Some strategies to optimize front-end operations include:

- Enabling online scheduling and paperless registration for patient convenience. This improves access.

- Gathering details on all insurance plans, including benefits, policies, and contact information during intake.

- Collecting applicable copays or pre-payments at check-in to offset collections work later.

- Integrating evidence-based screening tools and outcomes metrics into clinical documentation workflows to demonstrate value.

- Educating clinicians on compliant coding practices, common errors, and documentation specificity needed. Perform audits.

- Updating EHR templates regularly for efficient coding and higher evaluation & management (E&M) reimbursement.

- Staying current on annual coding changes and payer requirements. Adapt workflows accordingly.

- Leveraging coding analytics tools to identify documentation improvement opportunities by clinician.

Reflecting services accurately through detailed coding provides the foundation for the entire revenue cycle. Physician and clinician engagement is essential to improve documentation.

Financial Counseling and Collections

Patients bear more cost-sharing responsibility through high-deductible plans, making effective financial counseling and collections processes essential for rehabilitation clinic revenue integrity. Key elements include price transparency to provide estimates of out-of-pocket costs upfront to patients, which sets expectations. Eligibility verification, benefits investigation, and authorization confirmation prior to care are also important, as is reviewing deductibles and co-insurance obligations with patients during scheduling.

Offering payment plan options suitable to different circumstances and considering payment at the time of service for affordability can help manage patient financial responsibility. Explaining bills and statements clearly to patients, providing itemizations, and addressing concerns are also key. Making statements and collection notices consumer-friendly with plain language and multiple contact options improves the patient experience.

Training staff on patient-centric collections interactions that balance tact and tenacity is essential. Strategic segmentation of accounts to customize collection strategies based on dollar value and age can optimize results. Monitoring collector productivity and performance through call handle times, promise-to-pay rates, and other metrics ensures consistent execution.

While collections require diligence, a patient focus mitigates resentment and maintains community goodwill. Self-pay payment plans enable some realization from all patient encounters.

Revenue Integrity Focus

At its core, revenue cycle management in rehabilitation clinics involves consistently executing the fundamental *blocking and tackling* necessary to accurately capture and collect all value provided through patient care. This revenue integrity requires complete and precise documentation of diagnoses, interventions, supplies, equipment use, and minutes spent. Proper coding based on documentation specificity, medical necessity confirmation, and compliance best practices is also essential.

Timely charge entry matched directly to supporting clinical documentation is another critical component. Meticulous claim scrubbing to verify all components prior to submission, prompt payment posting when received, along with denial evaluation, and tenacious follow-up on unpaid claims and patient balances round out the key requirements.

With strong people, systems, and analytics in place, leaders must nurture a culture focused on diligence, compliance, efficiency, and teamwork to sustain revenue excellence. This uplifts financial performance while maintaining community trust.

Conclusion

In an increasingly complex reimbursement environment, disciplined revenue cycle management is imperative for rehabilitation clinics and departments. It entails both technical and cultural competence—from accurate coding to patient financial counseling. When thoughtfully designed and executed, the revenue cycle serves as a strategic asset that sustains clinical operations and enables fulfillment of the rehabilitation mission.

As Amanda and Max wrap up their revenue cycle mystery-solving session, she can't help but feel a sense of accomplishment. "Who knew that tracking down lost reimbursements could be so thrilling?" she grins, already planning a "Revenue Cycle Detective" themed escape room for her team.

Personal Reflection: Amanda realizes that revenue cycle management is not just about collecting payments; it's about ensuring the financial sustainability of her department and the hospital as a whole. She learns the importance of collaboration, attention to detail, and continuous process improvement. She commits to being a strong advocate for her team and to always putting patient care first, even as she works to optimize the revenue cycle.

Chapter Eleven

Leading Financial Change Management in Rehab

Amanda's on a mission to lead her team through the uncharted waters of financial change, and she's armed with a toolkit of leadership strategies and a sense of humor. In a heart-to-heart with another mentor, COO Dr. Jessica Wilson, Amanda prepares to unleash her inner motivational guru.

"Dr. Wilson, I feel like I'm trying to herd cats while juggling flaming batons," Amanda sighs, "How can I get everyone on board with these financial changes without causing a mutiny?"

Dr. Wilson smiles, "Ah, the art of leading change. It's like trying to convince a room full of toddlers that broccoli is the new ice cream. But with the right approach, you can get everyone excited about the journey ahead."

With Dr. Wilson's guidance, Amanda learns to communicate the "why" behind the changes, involve staff in the process, and celebrate the small victories along the way.

Implementing financial management strategies and best practices often requires significant changes within rehab organizations. As a leader, effectively navigating this change process is crucial for success. This chapter provides guidance on communicating with staff, overcoming resistance, and sustaining improvements to support the long-term financial health of your organization.

Communicating with Staff

Clear, consistent communication is essential when introducing financial changes. Follow these strategies to keep your staff informed and engaged:

- **Explain the "Why"**—Help staff to understand the reasons behind the financial changes. Connect the initiatives to your organization's mission, values, and goals.

- **Be Transparent**—Share relevant financial data and performance metrics with your team. Explain how their work contributes to the organization's financial success.

- **Use Multiple Channels**—Communicate through various methods, such as meetings, emails, newsletters, and one-on-one conversations, to ensure the message reaches everyone.

- **Listen and Seek Feedback**—Encourage open dialogue and actively listen to staff concerns and ideas. Incorporate their feedback into the change process when appropriate.

- **Celebrate Successes**—Recognize and celebrate milestones and achievements along the way to maintain momentum and staff engagement.

Overcoming Resistance

Change often encounters resistance, even when it's necessary for the organization's financial well-being. Use these approaches to address resistance and build support:

- **Identify Resistance Early**—Be proactive in recognizing signs of resistance, such as decreased productivity, negative comments, or lack of participation.

- **Understand Concerns**—Meet with resistant individuals to understand their concerns. Often, resistance stems from a fear of the unknown or perceived threats to their roles.

- **Provide Education and Training**—Offer training and resources to help staff gain the skills and knowledge needed to adapt to the financial changes.

- **Involve Staff in Problem-Solving**—Engage staff in identifying solutions and process improvements. Their involvement can increase buy-in and ownership of the changes.

- **Lead by Example**—Model the behaviors and attitudes you expect from your staff. Demonstrate your own commitment to financial best practices.

Sustaining Improvements

Sustaining financial improvements requires ongoing effort and commitment. Use these strategies to maintain progress and prevent backsliding:

- **Embed Changes into Operations**—Integrate financial best practices into daily workflows, job descriptions, and performance expectations.

- **Provide Ongoing Training**—Offer regular training and education to reinforce financial concepts and skills, particularly for new hires.

- **Monitor and Report Progress**—Regularly track and report on key financial metrics to ensure transparency and accountability.

- **Celebrate and Reward Success**—Recognize individuals and teams who consistently demonstrate financial best practices and contribute to the organization's financial goals.

- **Continuously Improve**—Encourage ongoing process improvement and innovation to further optimize financial performance.

Leading financial change management requires a combination of strong communication, empathy, and persistence. By engaging your staff, addressing resistance, and implementing strategies to sustain improvements, you can successfully navigate the change process and drive long-term financial success for your rehab organization.

Conclusion

Financial management is a critical skill for rehab leaders in today's complex healthcare environment. By mastering the concepts and strategies presented in this book, you'll be well-equipped to steer your organization towards financial stability and growth. Remember, financial success enables your organization to fulfill its mission of providing exceptional patient care and outcomes. Embrace your role as a financial leader and use your knowledge to create a long-lasting, positive impact on your staff, patients, and community.

> As Amanda wraps up her mentoring session with Dr. Wilson, she can't help but feel a sense of gratitude. "Who knew that leading change could be so rewarding?" she thinks, already planning a "Change Champion" recognition wall in the staff lounge.

Personal Reflection: Amanda realizes that leading financial change is not just about implementing new policies; it's about empowering her team to embrace innovation and to be active participants in the process. She learns the importance of clear communication, staff engagement, and celebrating successes along the way. She commits to being a transparent, supportive leader who always puts her team and patients first.

Afterword

As Amanda reflects on her whirlwind year as rehab department director, she can't help but smile at the memories of spreadsheets, acronyms, and the occasional dance party in the therapy gym. She's learned that leading a department isn't just about crunching numbers; it's about empowering her team to provide the best possible care for their patients.

In a final meeting with the hospital's leadership team, Amanda presents the department's impressive financial performance and the positive impact of her initiatives. The CFO, Mark Thompson, can't resist a little good-natured ribbing.

"Amanda, I have to hand it to you. When you first started, I wasn't sure if you were going to revolutionize the department or accidentally fund a mission to Mars. But you've proven that with a little creativity, a lot of hard work, and the occasional Dad joke, anything is possible."

Amanda realizes that being a successful rehab director is not just about managing finances; it's about leading with integrity, empathy, and a commitment to excellence. She learns the importance of continuous learning, collaboration, and staying true to her values. As she looks to the future, she knows that there will be new challenges and opportunities ahead, but she feels confident and prepared to tackle them head-on. With a grateful heart and a determined spirit, she steps forward, ready to lead her team to even greater heights.

Glossary

Accumulated depreciation tracks the total depreciation expense recorded for a fixed asset (e.g., equipment, buildings) over time, reducing its book value on the balance sheet.

Activity-based budgeting allocates costs based on client volume and service projections. More accurate for activity-driven operations.

Allowance for doubtful accounts reflects the estimated amount of accounts receivable that may not be collected due to bad debts.

Ambulatory Payment Classifications (APCs) are a government system for grouping similar outpatient services (OPPS) and setting fixed reimbursement rates for Medicare.

Anti-productivity challenges the focus on constant output, recognizing that seemingly unproductive activities like therapist self-care or preventative care can ultimately enhance long-term efficiency and patient outcomes.

Avoidable fixed costs are the fixed or overhead costs that could be eliminated or avoided if a particular service line or business unit was discontinued.

Balance billing occurs when providers bill patients for the difference between charge-based rates and what insurance paid. Discouraged, but still legal in some cases.

Balance Sheet provides a snapshot of assets, liabilities, and equity at a point in time. Assets must equal liabilities plus equity per the accounting equation. Comparing balance sheets over time shows changes in the business's financial position.

Benchmarking is comparing key ratios to industry benchmarks or past performance.

Breakeven analysis calculates the quantity of services a rehabilitation clinic or department must provide to cover its fixed costs.

Bundling combines payments for all providers and services involved in an episode of care into one lump sum amount. This incentivizes coordination and resource efficiency across the care continuum. Providers share cost savings achieved. Bundling is growing but still limited in use.

Capital budgets outline expected cash outflows for long-term investments like facilities, equipment, and IT systems. These require large upfront costs that then deliver value over many years.

Capitation pays healthcare providers a set dollar amount per member per month (PMPM) to cover all necessary services.

Case Mix Index (CMI) is a single number that reflects the average complexity and resource needs of patients treated at a healthcare facility, often used for setting reimbursement rates.

Cash-based clinics require patients to pay the therapist directly for services, bypassing insurance companies.

Ceteris paribus is a Latin phrase that generally means "all other things being equal." It acts as a shorthand indication of the effect one economic variable has on another, provided all other variables remain the same.

Collected revenue is the actual payment amounts received and is able to be recognized as revenue after providing services to patients.

Concierge medicine, also known as boutique or retainer medicine, is a healthcare model in which patients pay a membership or retainer fee to access enhanced and personalized medical care.

Contra asset account is a special type of asset account that has a credit balance (negative balance) instead of the usual debit balance associated with asset accounts.

Cost-benefit analysis is a systematic process for calculating and comparing the costs and benefits associated with different decision alternatives.

Current Procedural Terminology (CPT) defines the specific services or procedures performed by healthcare professionals.

Debt financing allows organizations to borrow funds that are repaid over time with interest through instruments like loans, bonds, and leases.

Debt management is the ability to manage leverage and meet debt obligations. Analyze the debt-to-equity ratio, debt ratio, and times interest earned.

Depreciation is the method of allocating the cost of a fixed asset over its useful life.

Diagnosis-Related Group (DRG) is a general classification system that groups patients with similar diagnoses, treatments, and resource use. It's used by various healthcare payers, including private insurers and government programs besides Medicare.

Differential cost analysis involves evaluating the varying costs between different choices.

Direct costs are expenses that can be directly attributed or traced to a specific patient, department, service, or cost center.

Economic Order Quantity (EOQ) formula is a mathematical model used to determine the optimal order quantity that minimizes the total inventory holding and ordering costs, balancing the trade-off between placing larger, less frequent orders and smaller, more frequent orders.

Efficiency represents how well assets are used. Measured using turnover ratios.

Equity financing involves selling ownership shares in the organization in return for capital, typically used by for-profit entities.

Fixed costs are expenses that remain constant regardless of volume or activity level.

Flexible budgeting creates multiple scenarios for different volume levels, allowing nimble responses to changing conditions.

Funded depreciation involves setting aside estimated depreciation dollars each year to self-fund upcoming replacement needs.

Gross Patient Service Revenue (GPSR) refers to the total charges or list prices billed for rehabilitation services provided before any reductions, contractual allowances, or adjustments.

Group Purchasing Organizations (GPOs) are entities that leverage the collective purchasing power of their members, such as healthcare providers or businesses, to negotiate lower prices and better terms with suppliers, manufacturers, and distributors.

Home Health Prospective Payment System (HH PPS) is a payment system used by Medicare to reimburse home health agencies (HHAs) for providing services to patients in their homes.

Hours worked is the time each therapist is being paid; this also referred to as billable hours, scheduled hours, or labor hours.

ICD-10 codes classify diagnoses and medical conditions.

Income Statement summarizes revenues earned and expenses incurred over a period of time. Shows whether the business operated at a profit or loss for that period. Can be prepared monthly and annually.

Incremental budgeting starts with the previous year's actual figures and then adds or subtracts modest increases or decreases to arrive at the budget. This is easy and fast but lacks rigor.

Individual-level productivity is how efficiently each therapist can treat those patients.

Indirect costs are expenses that cannot be directly tied to individual patients, services, or departments.

Inpatient hospital prospective payment system (IPPS) is the PPS Medicare uses to pay hospitals for inpatient services under preset rates.

Just-in-time (JIT) stock levels refer to an inventory management strategy where goods are received from suppliers just as they are needed for production or sale, minimizing inventory holding costs and reducing the risk of overstocking or stockouts.

Length of stay (LOS) measures the duration of a patient's hospital admission from the time of admission to discharge.

Liquidity is the ability to pay debts as they come due. Important ratios include the current ratio and days revenue outstanding.

Loss leader in rehab is a service offered at a price below cost, often to attract new patients or encourage them to use more profitable services later.

Medicaid is a joint federal-state program that provides health insurance coverage for low-income individuals and families.

Medicare is a federal health insurance program for individuals aged 65 or older, and some younger people with disabilities or specific conditions.

Medicare Severity-Diagnosis Related Groups (MS-DRGs) are patient classification systems that group patients into categories with similar diagnoses and resource use, used for setting Medicare reimbursement rates.

Net Patient Service Revenue (NPSR) is the actual revenue received and recorded after subtracting discounts, allowances, bad debt, and any other reconciling adjustments from the initial gross charges.

Operating budgets detail expected revenues and expenses for delivering day-to-day rehab services. This includes revenue projections, labor costs, facility expenses, materials, etc.

Operating surpluses involves allocating excess revenues over expenses to fund capital needs.

Outpatient Prospective Payment System (OPPS) is Medicare's prospective payment system focused on standardizing and bundling reimbursement for hospital outpatient services based on APC groups, rather than variable charges or costs.

Patient days measures the total number of days patients are admitted across all hospital beds during a given time period.

Patient service revenue includes payments for clinical services provided to patients. We can divide this into gross patient service revenue (GPSR) and net patient service revenue (NPSR).

Per diem **rate** is a fixed amount paid daily to determine reimbursement for services based on the duration of care or stay.

Philanthropy efforts secure donations, grants, sponsorships from individuals, foundations, corporations, and government entities to fund capital projects.

Practice location is a factor providers should consider when setting up practice in a new area; provider saturation data helps assess potential patient demand and competition.

Productivity is the efficient utilization of resources to achieve optimal patient outcomes, encompassing both individual provider efficiency and system—level resource allocation.

Profit is the excess of revenue over expenses.

Profitability is the ability to generate income relative to revenue and investment. Key ratios are profit margin, return on assets, and return on equity.

Prospective Payment System (PPS) sets a fixed reimbursement amount for a specific service beforehand, regardless of the actual cost or resources used.

Provider saturation refers to the density of healthcare providers offering a specific service within a defined geographic area relative to the number of patients who might benefit from those services.

Reserve for obsolescence is a contra asset account that reflects a potential reduction in value due to technological advancements or changing market conditions.

Resource allocation is distributing healthcare resources like equipment and personnel to address areas with provider shortages.

Return on Investment (ROI) is a performance measure used to evaluate the efficiency and profitability of an investment or compare the efficiency of different investments by calculating the ratio of the net profit (or loss) to the initial cost of the investment, usually expressed as a percentage.

Skilled Nursing Facility Prospective Payment System (SNF PPS) is a system used by Medicare to reimburse SNFs for the care provided to patients.

Statement of Cash Flows details cash inflows and outflows from operating, investing, and financing activities. Operating cash flow is particularly important for understanding profitability.

Step-variable costs are costs that remain constant within a range of activity but increase by a discrete amount when the activity exceeds that range, resulting in a step-like pattern when graphed.

Stockouts refer to situations where a product or item is temporarily unavailable or out of stock when a customer or client wants to purchase it, often leading to lost sales, reduced customer satisfaction, and potential damage to the company's reputation.

Sunk cost is an expense incurred in the past that we cannot recover.

System-level productivity is the efficiency with which a hospital or outpatient rehab clinic treats patients.

Unit costing analyzes the direct costs per unit of service (e.g., CPT code, patient day) and helps manage margins and optimize delivery costs.

Utilization refers to the percentage of total available time that fixed assets are operational and productive.

Value proposition budgeting starts with desired program outcomes and backs into required spending levels to meet those goals. Aligns budgets to strategy.

Variable costs are expenses that change in direct proportion to the volume of services.

Volume is the number of patients a therapist sees per day or per week in the clinic.

Zero-based budgeting (ZBB) builds budgets from scratch each cycle regardless of past spending. This is a time-consuming approach, but it avoids legacy inefficiencies.

Glossary

An epilogue is very similar to a prologue, but it occurs at the end of your story, though usually separate from the main plot. It might offer a glimpse of the future to share a sense of closure with your readers, or entice them to read the next in a series or collection.

Similar to the prologue, the epilogue should be placed in the main body content of your book and is therefore not technically back matter.

Acknowledgements

I would like to acknowledge the use of the AI tool, Claude.ai, which assisted me in generating ideas for case studies and providing feedback on drafts. While Claude.ai was helpful, all final decisions regarding content, style, and editing were my own.

.

www.ingramcontent.com/pod-product-compliance
Lightning Source LLC
Chambersburg PA
CBHW071605210326
41597CB00019B/3414